GW00985581

An Omelette

and three glasses of wine

En route with Citroëns

BY ANDREW BRODIE

Published in 2012 by Yellow Chevron Publishing
1st Edition
ISBN 978-0-9573441-0-5

Designed by Tilley Associates Ltd
www.tilleyassociates.com
Email: studio@tilleyassociates.com
Tel: +44 (0)207 720 2275

Printed and bound at Gomer Press Ltd
Llandysul, Ceredigion, SA44 4JL

Foreword

Evocative writing and stirring photography go together like food and wine. Put a fine writer and an imaginative photographer together in an interesting car on an appealing journey and you're going to get a captivating essay where words and images mesh perfectly. We can all, then, share in the magic as the adventure unfolds.

The writers in this book are masters of the car-and-road story art. They start with a love of cars, and a deep understanding of the enduring appeal of how and where cars can take you. They add in sharp observational skills and put their words down with enthusiasm, care and talent.

Phil Llewellin (23 October 1940 - 1 July 2005), who wrote most of these stories, showed in his own book — 'The Road To Muckle Flugga' (Haynes) — just what a charming and sensitive writer he was. Cars and places, and the people he met along the way, were his subjects of choice and he enriched immensely the worlds of motoring and travel journalism. Alongside his skill as a wordsmith, Phil was a painstaking researcher. You will find his tales are journeys of discovery in more ways than one.

Like his fellow storytellers in this book — Paul Horrell and Dale Drinnon; and Andrew Brodie, the Citroëniste who provided the cars and accompanied them — Phil could not have wished for a finer photographer and driving companion than Martyn Goddard.

Wendy Harrop, renowned Art Director of CAR magazine from 1975 to 1980, says of Martyn: "He is amazingly resourceful. He knows his craft through and through. He always knows the latest techniques, technology and developments — every trick in the book. He has a wonderful eye for composition. He is one of those photographers who can photograph any subject. You can ask Martyn to photograph a car, a building, a landscape or a superstar and know that he will always take a fantastic photograph. To top it off, he's always cheerful and fun to work with."

Moreover, Martyn is a Citroën lover. He has owned two SMs. So every picture in this book has an extra infusion of insight and passion.

It's a book filled with stories and photographs of the highest order, all celebrating important and fascinating cars.
—

MEL NICHOLS, LONDON 2012

Introduction

Turning my enthusiasm for classic cars from a hobby into a living was definitely the best career decision I ever made. It has led me to meet some amazing people, have some great friendships, and not coincidentally, take part in a number of exceptional and extremely enjoyable photographic and journalistic road trips. This book is a collection of some of the magazine articles resulting from these adventures.

Having thought out and planned a trip that would be of general interest, as well as highlighting a particular vehicle, we worked seriously hard getting the photos and stories into place, often against considerable difficulty from the elements and happenstance. Early starts, long days, flexibility and often a fair bit of luck were essential. It was inspiring to me to meet these professionals and witness their dedication to getting the job done right. The fact that they also made the work fun is among the many reasons I am keen to share the memories.

We were furthermore very fortunate in being largely left alone to tell the stories in our own way and, due to special circumstances, they are unique. These same circumstances also make them sadly unlikely to ever be repeated. I think you will find that these articles capture the atmosphere of the regions to which we travelled and the character of the people we met as well as the qualities of the cars. I believe, too, that these stories might just encourage you into adventures of your own.

I hope you enjoy this book and come back to re-read it many times, as I have done the original articles.

—

ANDREW BRODIE, LONDON 2012

Biographies

ANDREW BRODIE

Andrew Brodie's Citroën passion began in 1972, when convinced by his chums to buy a new GS, and life was never again the same. He changed from computing to working on Citroëns many years ago. Andrew still owns the SMs and the red DS, amongst other cars. He does have additional interests, such as an English Electric Lightning T5, and is still involved in the International Wine & Food Society. Being retired now he never gets a day off, but tries to improve his questionable historic rallying skills, in the SM of course, when he needs to relax.

MARTYN GODDARD

Martyn studied photography at Harrow College of Art and after graduating assisted various leading photographers before going freelance. He became part of the New Wave music scene of the seventies, working with acts such as Blondie, The Jam and The Cure to name a few. Invited to contribute to the Sunday Telegraph Magazine he was assigned to portrait and feature shoots and at CAR magazine he worked on automotive and travel stories. He became a Fellow of the British Institute of Professional Photography in1987. In recent years he has moved to a digital platform, becoming an active photo-blogger and content provider supplying a comprehensive service producing travel features and images for syndication.

PHIL LLEWELLIN

Phil Llewellin was a journalist and writer who, for 40 years, translated his passion for cars and travel into award-winning articles for publications in the UK and abroad, including Car Magazine, The Observer, the Daily Telegraph, Truck magazine, The Independent, Car & Driver, and Automobile Magazine. Described as "one of the best motoring writers, if not the best, of the past four decades", his wide-ranging and often humorous work encompassed not just vehicles and global travel but aspects of history, engineering, geography and culture. Born in Oswestry, Shropshire, he died of a heart attack in 2005 whilst on holiday in Croatia. A collection of his writing, 'The Road to Muckle Flugga', was published in 2004.

DALE DRINNON

A native-born and raised American and long-time British resident, Dale Drinnon's first car was a very second-hand Fiat 850 Spider, and he's been addicted to cars of distinctive style and character ever since. His current daily-driver is a much-beloved Xantia V6 Exclusive, purchased, of course, from Andrew Brodie himself, with whom he has also shared many enjoyable meals and even the occasional glass of wine. A former businessman, mechanic and historic racer, Dale writes about cars and anything vaguely car-related for a variety of publications worldwide.

PAUL HORRELL

Paul Horrell was deputy editor of the lamented British magazine Supercar & Classics when he undertook a French expedition in Andrew Brodie's GS Birotor. It didn't cure him of a lifelong love of GSs, and soon after he bought a GSX3. Since then he's been mostly writing about modern cars, becoming a senior writer on CAR Magazine until 2003, when he switched to freelancing. Now he's Consultant Editor and columnist for BBC TopGear Magazine, and European Editor for Motor Trend (USA), and also a juror for Car of the Year. He's widely respected among his peers for his analysis of the car industry as well of cars themselves.

Contents

French Lessons

Or how Phil Llewellin got to grips with Citroën's eccentric yet charming SM while taking in some Norman military history and much of the area's produce

Words by Phil Llewellin
Pictures by Martyn Goddard

He knows these cars well enough to be on first-name
terms with every nut, bolt and widget

récy-en-Ponthieu was the most appropriate place, we agreed, because it was there that a much earlier generation of British visitors proved capable of mastering the French. With luck, their spirits would bless my first attempt to drive what must be the most unconventional of all grand tourers, a formidably big car synonymous with strange steering and hyper-sensitive brakes. Andrew Brodie had revealed the 1973 Citroën SM's mile-eating potential on the N1, south of Calais, and while galloping along the minor road to Crécy at a crisp, confident 100mph.

But he knows these cars well enough to be on first-name terms with every nut, bolt and widget, and is one of the few people to

have hurled an SM around the Goodwood racetrack. Brodie is a true believer, and a great character. He runs Hypertronics, the North London business that specialises in Citroëns. The sight of an ancient 2CV or D-series does for him what salacious memories of old Brigitte Bardot movies still do for me. No item of equipment, on this 800 mile jaunt to Normandy and back, was more important than Brodie's blue sweater which has the Double Chevron stitched into its chest. In yellow, of course. Like all dyed-in-the-wool Citroënistes, he regards the change to a red trademark as the most shameful event since Peugeot bailed the company out in 1974.

Our journey to "the vasty fields of France" started at Mr. Photographer Goddard's home in London. Goddard runs a Citroën

Dyane, a 16-valve BX 19GTi and, would you believe, an SM. This would have been akin to muscling in on a family affair were it not for my wife's transport being a 2CV. Brodie, whose background includes aeronautical engineering and computers, talked about his enthusiasm for the marque while wasting no time on the road to Dover: "In the good old days, Citroën was the one manufacturer willing to take a completely fresh look at familiar problems. The bug bit while I covered 100,000 hard miles in a GS estate. Then came the 1220 version. I remember passing an Elan in that, on the M5 south of Birmingham, despite having the tailgate open and a three-piece suite in the back. Silly, really, but the little bugger just wanted to keep going faster."

The SM epitomises Citroën's mould-breaking philosophy. Launched at the 1970 Geneva Motor Show, it features front-wheel drive, fully independent and self-levelling hydropneumatic suspension, plus driver-selectable height adjustment, headlights that swivel with the exceptionally high-geared steering, and four disc brakes.

Maserati, acquired by Citroën two years before the SM's debut, provided the 2.67 litre V6, four-cam engine which was derived from the Maserati Indy's 4.1 litre V8. Key figures quoted in the owner's manual include 178bhp at 5500rpm, and 171lb ft of torque at 4000. Bosch fuel injection replaced the triple Webers in 1972. A year later, Maserati produced a 3.0 litre to complement the optional Borg-Warner automatic box.

All these good things came together in a two-door body that was aerodynamically excellent, even by today's slippery standards, but big and heavy. Sixteen feet long, and just over six wide, an SM additionally burdened with air conditioning tips the scales at around 1.5 tons when empty. Brodie believes his Citroën to be the only one in Britain equipped with the optional glass fibre composite wheels, which are less than half the weight of the steel variety and can withstand far more severe impacts. The only snag, he says, is that they break rather than bend.

We spent the night at the Cliffe Court Hotel, literally no more than a first-to-second shift from the dock gates, and boarded Sealink's 'St Christopher' an hour before the sun heaved itself over the horizon. Alongside us was a flatbed laden with a Ford tractor. This was shunted hard enough to damage the trailer parked behind, but the SM emerged with panels and paintwork intact. Brodie donned the sweater before putting the first batch of fast miles beneath wheels whose six-inch rims are shod with Michelin 205/70 VR 15 XWX rubber.

Crécy was the first name on the hit list,

This was shunted hard enough to damage the trailer parked behind, but the SM emerged with panels and paintwork intact

At speed on a Route
Nationale
—
On a back street in Montreuil

À vitesse sur une Route
Nationale
—
Sur une petite rue à
Montreuil

but we took a quick look at Montreuil, a picturesque hilltop town which has wide-ranging views, cobbled streets and massive fortifications built by one of that art's great masters, Sebastian le Prestre de Vauban, a 17th Century Marshal of France. Goddard's need to be on the qui vive for Nikon targets relegated me to the rear accommodation, which must be fine for children or ladies of not more than their sex's average height, but proved quite a tight fit for six feet of overweight adult male. Although there was a little more headroom than expected, space for my legs, which are short, was at a premium, even when Goddard slid his leather-trimmed seat as

far forward as it would go. The boot also lacks the room you associate with a car which is almost as long as a Jaguar XJ6. But few cars in general and grand tourers in particular, can match the Citroën SM's ride comfort. Notes in handwriting as legible as it will ever be were jotted down while Brodie belted over railway crossings and potholes that should have made the pen leap like a seismograph needle during a major earthquake. Heading for Crécy, Brodie said: "I remember going along a road just like this in a Triumph Stag. It was crashing and banging and jostling all over the place at 60. We're doing almost 100, but you'd never guess it." »

Phil checking the days route

Phil contrôle la voie du jour

Born and bred on the Welsh Marches, where he still lives, the chronicler of this foray had never before made time to visit Crécy-en-Ponthieu. Many of the archers who fought there on August 26, 1346, came from my part of the world to fight for King Edward the Third and his son, Edward the Black Prince. A wooden tower, built recently by Les Amis des Vieux Moulins, marks the site of the ridge-top windmill from which England's monarch was able to see the entire battlefield.

Here, as at Agincourt in 1415, French knights charged beneath a sky loud with the deadly music of clothyard arrows from longbows plucked by yokels paid sixpence a day. Long pointed 'bodkins', whose quality has astonished modern metallurgists, pierced the noble armour. Barbed heads plunged deep into equine and human flesh. Robert Hardy's truly superb 'Longbow' book, published by Patrick Stephens in 1976, tells how an archer was "very lightly

esteemed" if he could not fire a dozen arrows in a minute, and make each one hit its target at a range of 240 yards.

The Black Prince later awarded rights of pasture and turf-cutting to his faithful bowmen. They included the Black Army of Llantrisant, a company of Welshmen whose direct descendents may still apply to be enrolled as freemen of the borough. Each claim must trace the applicant's lineage right back to the ancestor who fought at the great battle.

Time to move on, now without Brodie's expert hands at the wheel. I think about that "very lightly esteemed" quote while adjusting the SM's leather-trimmed seat. Cushion and backrest form more of a curve than an angle, and the articulation point is around hip level. There's not much in the way of lateral support should the novice generate more than 0.001g while cornering. Oval dials embrace the 160mph speedometer, the clock, and a tachometer

red-lined from 6500 to 8000. Enough warning lights to shame Blackpool's famous illuminations supplement the major and minor instruments. All are rendered insignificant by a red blob looking like the "eye" of HAL, the computer that caused all the trouble in Arthur C Clarke's '2001: A Space Odyssey'. When that flashes, you STOP.

Maserati's V6 settles down to a rich, thick, bubbling tickover while I check the mirrors, and make sure there's nothing too quirky about the shift pattern of this left-hand-drive car's five-speed gearbox. The lever's base looks rather like a chromed ashtray, but the slots are where you expect them to be, and first engages sweetly. This is not a light, quick shift, but by the end of the trip it has earned high marks for smoothness and precision. It conveys an impression of real, carved-from-solid machinery, not a bucket of nervous cogs, shafts and bearings.

Getting onto the road from the medieval battlefield's car park involved driving straight ahead for about twice the SM's length, then making a right-angle turn. I moved off just a touch faster than intended, and tweaked the wheel. Brodie and Goddard laughed as the Citroën attempted to bite its own tail, then lurched in the opposite direction as their chauffeur tried to correct his mistake, and lurched again before directional stability was achieved. Predictably, I had been taken unawares by the VariPower steering's gearing — it takes just two turns from lock to lock — and the system's almost incredible low-speed sensitivity.

Steering effort increases with speed, but getting in tune with the system's gearing takes a little time. South of Abbeville, where the road spears through woodland, I intended easing out to overtake while travelling at about 90mph. The SM described more of a zig-zag than a gentle

Maserati's V6 settles down to a rich, thick, bubbling tickover while I check the mirrors

The battlefield at Crécy

—

Crécy battlefield sign

—

Llewellin at speed

Le champ de bataille de Crécy

—

Signe du champ de bataille de Crécy

—

Llewellin à vitesse

Museum in Clères
—
Visiting a dealer in Honfleur, with an SM on display inside
—
Inside museum at Clères

Musée de Clères
—
Visite d'un concessionnaire à Honfleur, avec un SM en vue a l'intérieur
—
A l'intérieur du musée à Clères

curve, darting left and right in response to far more movement than the wheel required. This is a car you can steer at high speed by flexing your wrists, and park using your little finger to exert gentle pressure on the wheel's single spoke. Citroën's braking system is even less conventional. Activated by a rubber mushroom, not a pedal, it responds to pressure rather than movement. Reacting to situations as you would in an ordinary car can project dentures into the windscreen, and make you wonder if Citroën intended 'SM' to be shorthand for 'somersault'.

Despite all this, and the car's formidable bulk, the Brodie Tours' trainee driver was feeling far more confident than expected when we stopped for a lunchtime snack in Blangy. Brodie, a member of the Wine and Food Society, ordered a platter of haute cuisine sausage and chips. The café sold magazines as well as food, offering choices that ranged from 'L'Automobile' to such incredibly mind-improving journals as 'Revues Pornos de Luxe'.

We pushed on to Clères, where jovial Jackie Pichon's motor museum, packed with French cars and a multi-national armoured

division of military vehicles, stands across the road from his other interest, the Auberge du Cheval Noir. The stars of the museum include a wonderfully rakish 1912 Gregoire Sport Type 70SS, a replica of the vast Renault that set a new 24 hour world record in 1926, and a splendid 1926 Voisin which has "coupé chauffeur" coachwork. Among other marques recalled here are Lafitte, Chenard-Walcker, Delage, Ballot, Facel, Léon Bollée, and Panhard et Levassor. We also admired the neat little 1934 "cabriolet tres rare" Citroën 7B coupé before Brodie moved back into the SM's cockpit. Clear skies gave way to heavy rain as he skirted rush-hour Rouen, crossed the Seine, and headed in the general direction of Caen. Despite a reputation for understeer, the SM cornered hard enough in the wet for yours truly, huddled in the back, to be more than a little grateful for the central armrest.

Monsieur Michelin's invaluable guide to France suggested the Auberge du Vieux Puits in Pont-Audemer as a good bet for the night, but it shuts the doors on Tuesdays. We eventually homed in on the Hotel du Clos St Gatien, just north of Pont l'Eveque. The rooms had only just enough space to swing a Manx kitten, but all you need is

a bed after a good meal preceded by huge glasses of Normandy golden gold cocktail. This soothing blend of orange juice and grenadine would be harmless were it not for the apricot liqueur, gin and Calvados.

Next morning, giving thanks for the sun's return, we nipped up to Honfleur, an ancient fishing port that's almost too pretty. Brodie was far more impressed by the 1975 SM spotted in a Citroën garage on the outskirts. The price worked out at just under £9000: back in Blighty, quoth the guru, the top whack is now about £12,000. Thirty grand is nearer the mark for one of the convertibles built by Chapron, because total production can almost be counted on the fingers of one hand.

We headed south, following quiet roads through tranquil country famous for cheese. Pont l'Eveque of course, Livarot and Camembert. According to my father, who reckons France would be perfect if the French started playing cricket, Paris has a by-law that makes it an offence to carry Livarot in a taxi. It's great stuff, but does tend to smell like old socks. Brodie adopted the sort of voice used by American TV commentators when we reached

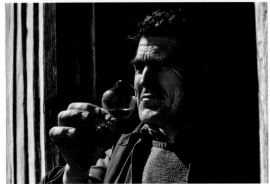

Citroën's unique grand tourer is not a car one would care to drive long and hard on really demanding roads, certainly not with the owner on board

Vimoutiers: "Despite her handicap, this plucky 18th Century French girl invented what many consider to be the world's finest cheese," he intoned. We were looking at a headless statue of Marie Harel. Closer inspection of the inscription revealed it to have been decapitated when Uncle Sam's liberating army passed this way in 1944. A complete statue, presented to the town by cheesemakers from Van Wert, Ohio, stands in the square, and there's also a monument to Marie Harel on the lane that skirts nearby Camembert. This is a tiny village where a few timber-framed farm buildings huddle close to a fine old church of honey-coloured stone. Brodie spots an almost equally ancient Citroën Ami: "One of God's more stylish creations," he smiles.

By then I had become accustomed to the SM's initially daunting combination of size, steering and brakes, and was enjoying the solid, stimulating rasp that is the Maserati engine's battle cry at high revs. Citroën's unique grand tourer is not a car one would care to drive long and hard on really demanding roads, certainly not with the owner on board, but it wafts and weaves along interesting, traffic-free by-ways considerably and consistently faster than expected. Dividing time into distance invariably reveals your estimated average speed to be way below the true figure. Few qualities are more important in a car.

Drawbacks? Punctuating cruising at around 80mph with ventures into three-figure territory does tend to do for the francs what King Alfred did to the cakes. We averaged

Old Camembert sign

—

M Claude, Calvados producer

—

William the Conquerer statue in Falaise

—

Pegasus Bridge memorial, British WW2 tank

Vieux signe Camembert

—

M Claude producteur de Calvados

—

Statue de Guillaume le Conquérant à Falaise

—

Mémorial du pont de Pegasus, blinde Britannique de WW2

19.2mpg overall, but even that gave the SM a range of almost 400 miles. Twenty gallons, less a pint or two, can be squirted into the tank. Additional fluid was loaded aboard when Brodie suggested following a "cidre, pommeau, Calvados" sign on the road between Vimoutiers and Trun. It guided us to the lovely old farmhouse, cupped in a serene valley, where these local specialities are brewed by Olivier Claude and his wife. Liking what we tasted, we departed laden with bottles. We also vowed to return, because the nearby cottage — pretty enough to have come straight from the pages of a fairy tale — is rented out under the admirable gites ruraux scheme.

A café in Trun served a three-course lunch, plus wine and coffee, for £5 a head. Then it was on to Falaise. In the cobbled Place

Guillaume le Conquerant, the Hotel de Ville and Eglise Sainte Trinite overlook what has to be one of Europe's most dramatic equestrian statues. Born here in 1027, the rider on the rampant charger became Duke William of Normandy before nipping over to Hastings in 1066. Much closer to our own time, Falaise gave its name to the bloody "pocket" where the Allies finally crushed German resistance in Normandy after the D-Day landings.

Guided by Goddard's navigation, the team's historian then punched hard for our overnight stop at the secluded Manoir de la Roche Torin. Selected from the Hotels Relais du Silence brochure, this proved to be a beautifully furnished and decorated watering hole dating from towards the end of the last century. From the dining room

there were breathtaking views of the sun setting behind Mont St Michel's pinnacled grandeur. Brodie marked the moment by ordering a 1983 Gewurztraminer and a 1974 St Émilion Chateau Haut Simard. Just about the only thing the hotel lacked was a snug little bar in which to relax while sniffing a post-prandial Calvados.

Following what the French call breakfast, Goddard scored bonus points for guiding us to the outskirts of Caen on a superb country road whose long straights and gentle sweeps, punctuated by a few wiggly sections, were ideally suited to the SM's character. Goddard, who hails from Buckinghamshire, swelled with pride when we reached the Pegasus Bridge, between Caen and the sea. It was here that gliders of the Sixth Airborne Division landed men »

Mont St Michel at sunset
—
Parked near Mont St Michel

Mont St Michel au coucher
du soleil
—
Stationné près de Mont
St Michel

On the beach near Mont St
Michel

—

Marcel Labourde with his old
2CV van

—

Paratrooper memorial at
Ste Mère-Eglise

Sur la plage, au matin, près
de Mont St Michel

—

Marcel Labourde avec sa
vieille camionnette 2CV

—

Mémorial de parachutiste à
Ste Mère-Eglise

The quintessentially French driver, a delightful old chap by the name of Marcel Labourde, was amazed and delighted by all the fuss

of the 'Ox and Bucks' regiment in the last minutes of June 5, 1944. The night was dark, and the winds strong, but the troops landed within a stone's throw of their objective. Their task? To secure the D-Day invasion's eastern flank. Lord Lovat's men, marching behind piper Bill Millin, reached the bridge at the end of the Longest Day's longest morning. Lovat apologised to Major John Howard. He was two minutes behind schedule.

Apart from Ste Mère-Eglise, where a wounded American paratrooper survived after dangling from the church spire for several hours, our last stop was in Bayeux, the first French town to be liberated. The world and his wife visit Bayeux to explore its ancient streets, visit the Norman cathedral, and see the tapestry made to commemorate William the Conqueror's victory. But what grabbed the attention of Brodie and Goddard was a 1955 Citroën 2CV powered, if that's the word, by a 405cc version of the air-cooled two-potter.

The quintessentially French driver, a delightful old chap by the name of Marcel Labourde, was amazed and delighted by all the fuss. But the beaming, red-cheeked little man lost points by asking if your reporter had hit the nearby beaches on D-Day. I wasn't born until the end of 1940. It was time to go home. Driving fast between stops for French food and tonsil tonic is a lot of fun, but it can make you look like the portrait Dorian Gray kept hidden in the attic. ◆

Outside lunch Hotel in Trun
—
Phil at lunch
—
Brodie and Llewellin
discussing driving techniques
—
A 1988 Brodie

Exterieur de l'Hôtel à Trun
ou nous avons déjeune
—
Phil au déjeuner
—
Brodie et Llewellin discutent
des techniques de conduit
—
Un Brodie de 1988

FOOTNOTE

Although Martyn was already a friend, I did not know Phil and set out on this first venture rather nervous in the presence of the famous journalist. However, we quickly crystallised into a team. Phil was enquiring, interested in the car and its history, meticulous with his notes and, above all, great company.

The Calvados maker's portrait was taken shortly after I spotted his sign by the side of the road, and shows how opportunities need to be taken (the Calvados was good!). In those days Citroën dealers still knew about the classic Citroëns, hence the SM in the showroom.

We spotted the 2CV when we were walking in the centre of Caen and we set off stressed we'd lose it. Fortunately he was driving at a very sedate pace, as befitted the ages of car and driver, so we caught up (very out of breath) just as he parked. The 'Sunset at Mont St Michel' photograph is also illustrative of seizing the moment, as Martyn abandoned his dinner (a good one, too) to run off and capture it.

Last but not least, my attempt at strangling Phil was jokingly staged after he had been driving toward Mont St Michel along the top of a dyke at high speed. We suddenly realised the cross-road we were approaching was a good 20 feet below our level, and our local gravity was close to zero as he emergency braked over the humpback down to the crossing!

—

ANDREW BRODIE 2012

Charge de Gaul

*Phil Llewellin and friends cut a rapid swathe through France
in one of the greatest saloons ever, a Citroën DS*

Words by Phil Llewellin
Pictures by Martyn Goddard

On a lock bridge of the
Burgundy canal

—

Parked in a Chablis vineyard

Sur un pont écluse du canal
de Bourgogne

—

Stationné dans un vignoble
de Chablis

In 1955, a cheering, exuberantly enthusiastic crowd besieged Citroën's stand at the Paris Motor Show. The future had arrived in the astonishing shape of the DS19, a shark-nosed saloon that has been rightly hailed as a major landmark in the automobile's history. Features that made its rivals look like throw-backs to the chariot-and-charger age included advanced aerodynamics — to make the most of what was essentially a pre-war engine — inboard disc brakes for the front wheels, an entirely novel self-levelling hydropneumatic suspension, and, of course, the front-wheel-drive layout that had been a Citroën speciality since 1934.

The people who flocked to the stand didn't just goggle, gasp and gape. Citroën's reputation for delivering the avant-garde engineering goods helped account for 749 firm orders within 45 minutes of the newcomer's sensational debut. By the end of the day, the total had topped 12,000. The whole of the following year's planned production had been accounted for.

Cars for the British market were assembled at Citroën's factory in Slough until 1966. One of the last, GBL 666C, was sold by the importer's Reading dealer on

10 September 1965. The total on-the-road price was £1664/13/9d. What is now an amazingly low-mileage car remained with the original buyer until 1968. Twenty years later, the second owner sold it to Andrew Brodie, who regards yesterday's Citroëns as the greatest things to come out of France since Dom Perignon invented champagne. His business, Hypertronics, restores them on the Sapcote Trading Estate in Willesden, London NW10.

Brodie, whose qualifications include membership of the International Wine and Food Society, suggested giving the 'Day Ess' an opportunity to stretch its legs on French roads. How would a 25-year-old example of a 35-year-old design, propelled by an engine whose roots go right back to the Traction Avant of 1934, stand up to a long weekend involving a four-figure mileage? Photographer 'Jean Luc' Goddard and I accepted the offer with alacrity. Brodie's credentials as a first-class travelling companion had been proved during a few days in Normandy with a Citroën SM, chronicled in the August 1988 issue of 'Supercar Classics'. Chris Morrow, who speaks fluent French, volunteered to be our interpreter.

Thursday

This is the life! Stagger out of makeshift bed in Goddard's studio at five o'cursing clock. Brodie arrives in mind-boggling DS that has clocked only 15,909 miles from new. He fills Gasthof Goddard's breakfast room with doom-laden talk of dodgy driveshafts, how incredibly complicated the gear linkage is — something about ball bearings in a holed tube — then switches to such light-hearted topics as the SM's manually tensioned secondary chains. Your reporter, looking even blanker than usual, explains that, at this hour, he's incapable of concentrating on anything more technical than crunching cornflakes.

Boot swallows personal luggage, plus Goddard's photographic equipment, without too much trouble. But finding room for a few cases of wine will be a problem. Brodie drives, with Gallic panache, while Goddard navigates us out of London. Morrow and Llewellin stretch legs and relax in the exceptionally spacious rear compartment. Wave to worker ants, crawling into the city, as blue Citroën cruises eastward at 75-80mph.

"Top speed was 101, according to the Autocar road test," says Brodie. "But the old 1.9 litre engine has a reputation for throwing rods if you get too enthusiastic. This is the high compression version" — he interjects a mocking laugh — "so we're talking about 8.5 to one and all of 83bhp on tap at 4500revs. Sounds like a middle-aged bumble bee when you put your foot down."

Must have crossed the Dover-Calais ditch literally hundreds of times, but this is the first trip by hovercraft. This 18-year-old member of Hoverspeed's fleet is named after Sir Christopher Cockerell, who filed his first cushion-of-air craft patent in 1955. The ramp angle gives Brodie an excuse to remind us that DS features — carried over to the CX and today's Car of the Year XM

100 mph on the Autoroute near Reims

—

Inside-outside view of RHD steering wheel

—

The DS in the Place Vendôme, Paris

160 kph sur l'autoroute près de Reims

—

Vue extérieur/interieur du volant conduite a droite

—

Les DS de la Place Vendôme, Paris

— include a body that rises or falls through umpteen inches as you move a lever inside. Cars are strapped to the deck. Goddard recalls brother-in-law, who used to work for Hoverspeed and once saw an XJ6 hit the roof during a rough crossing. Depart right on time... but return four minutes later, with a skirt problem. Commendably swift transfer to standby craft, but soon after,

I realise that these crossings are too short for a proper breakfast to be served. Fortunately, the International Wine and Food Society's representative produces a package of home-made rosbif sandwiches as the Swift tackles what Admiral Sir Francis Beaufort's scale classifies as a near gale. The captain says: "I hope you're having a reasonably comfortable crossing."

Parked alongside a section
of the Burgundy canal

Stationné à côté d'une
section du canal de
Bourgogne

Your reporter, looking even blanker than usual, explains that at this hour he's incapable of concentrating on anything more technical than crunching cornflakes

Back on land, interpreter and chronicler comment on excellent visibility from back seat before settling down to peruse the Financial Times. Brodie drives to within about 70 miles of Paris, then hands over to me as rain starts to fall.

My half of the split-bench front seat lacks much in the way of shape, but feels almost armchair comfortable. Soft seats tend not to be good for the back — mine has been giving trouble for years — so wonder what the end-of-day report will be. Big, single-spoke wheel, spiral-bound in black plastic. Curved dash, flanked by large air vents and demister bleeds for side windows, has rectangular speedometer, plus water temperature and fuel gauges. Seven identical knobs would be anonymous had previous owner not applied such stick-on clues as "WSW" for windscreen wipers. Four-speed gearbox's cogs are juggled by a lever on left of steering column. The shift pattern is easy to remember, though: first is third, second fourth, third first and fourth second if compared with a conventional four-on-the-floor shift layout.

The only place for the left foot is under the clutch, because the old Traction motor is set far enough back for Brodie to nominate the DS as the first mid-engined five-seater. The clutch itself travels as far as Marco Polo, but engages sweetly just before knee reaches ear. Must remember that the black rubber mushroom of a brake pedal responds to pressure, not a common-or-garden car's umpteen inches of movement.

Fast-moving traffic thickens as we start negotiating the Boulevard Peripherique. What its owner describes as "the full two bob watch" of an engine lacks mid-range muscle for battling with six lanes of big-city belligerents. Car also lacks exterior mirrors, so rely on peripheriqueal vision, supplemented by Brodie's anguished gasps, to avoid side-swiping the locals while responding to last-gasp instructions from Martyn the Map.

Average 64mph from Calais to mid-afternoon lunch on autoroute near Orleans. Brimming 14 gallon tank reveals DS to have averaged 30.1mpg over 349 miles. Three-course meal for about £8 includes apple tart notable for pastry tough enough to protect the space shuttle's nose. Push on to tranquil little spa town of Neris-les-Bains. Hotel Mercurc has splendid fin de siècle facade — as have many other buildings — but the interior is modern, anonymous. Amazed by complete absence of twinges after 478 mile journey. Cross road to wonderfully ornate casino's restaurant. Exceptionally effusive welcome probably linked with fact that we appear to be the night's only potential gamblers. Brodie and Morrow treat Goddard and Llewellin to £30 bottle of Margaux. Corsican casino boss adds to the merriment by offering his British guests a buckshee bottle of champagne; "No bad feelings about Napoleon and Waterloo!" he chortles.

Friday

Why are we right in the centre of France? To visit Pierre Bardinon, one of the galaxy's greatest Ferrari fans, for a Super-cars I Have Known interview (SCC, January). He lives near Aubusson, and has a two-mile race track in his back garden. Before reaching there, stop to inspect Citroën ID19, parked on verge with for sale sign on windscreen. Turns out to be a 1961 model that has covered 60,000 miles. Alphonse is asking the equivalent of just less than £2000. Brodie and Goddard exchange glances — the snapper is another Citroëniste — but I remind them that we have a job to do: "Punctuality is the politeness of kings," quoting no less appropriate an authority than King Louis XVIII of France.

Bardinon's mind-blowing collection, beautifully housed in an old farm building of almost golden granite, includes a short-wheelbase 250GT, two 250GTOs and four Le Mans winners. The first car he ever owned, just after the war, was nothing less than a Type 35B Bugatti. He's very anxious not to be depicted as having bought the Ferraris as investments. Most were acquired years ago, when old racers were 10-a-penny by today's crazy standards. Why collect then? Because right from childhood he had been fascinated by top-quality high-performance cars. He has raced and hill-climbed. Pierre Bardinon is nothing if not an enthusiast. His heart's in the right place, and he has also been blessed with a great

sense of humour. Within minutes we're chatting and laughing like old friends.

Would we like to join him and his wife for a light lunch? How kind. Would we like an aperitif of some sort? How very kind. Champagne? How very, very kind. Brodie is handed the short straw — "Guess who's driving for the rest of the day" — as corks pop from bottles of 1982 Moët en Chandon. Sit at a huge granite table, made for a great 19th Century exhibition, whose top alone weighs almost two tons. "Apple with apple" is Bardinon's suggestion for dessert. This turns out to be the best tarte au pomme I've ever savoured, accompanied by old calvados whose softness belies a

kick like a mule. The light lunch ends at four o'clock.

We're hoping to reach Chalon-sur-Saone, about 200 miles away on iffy roads, in time to investigate a restaurant good enough to win one of the Michelin guide's coveted stars. Brodie determines to show how swiftly the venerable Citroën can be hustled along, even on wet roads. There's a lot of roll. Chris Morrow abandons ship in Moulins. This is not a reflection on Brodie's cavalier wheel-manship: he's catching the rattler to Paris. God willing, we'll all meet up there on Sunday. Reach hoped-for destination exactly four hours after bidding the Bardinons farewell. Chauffeur says;

"Passengers are disrespectfully invited to contribute to the BBC — Brodie Beverage Collection — before leaving the bus."

Leave luggage in pleasantly old-style Hotel St Jean, overlooking River Saone, then walk through rain to Hotel St Georges' Michelin-starred scofferie. Excellent dinner for as little as £11, in my case, ends Marc de Bourgogne — also known as Ariane rocket fuel — distilled from skins, stalks and pipe left after grapes have been pressed.

Brodie driving Morrow and Llewellin in DS19

—

On the road north from Beaune

—

Brodie conduit Morrow et Llewellin dans sa DS19

—

En route au nord de Beaune

Saturday

Joseph Nicephore Niépce, 'Inventeur de la Photographie' was born in 1765. Superb museum dedicated to him is a two-minute walk from our hotel. Spend most of morning fascinated by vast collection of cameras spanning 150 years. Leica, Mick-a-Matic, Globuscope, Hasselblad used on the moon, amazing little turn-of-century spy cameras, huge 1940-vintage Japanese device for air-to-ground work, Victorian box cameras big enough to prompt jokes about planning permission… you name it. Wonderful 19th Century images are displayed in salons recalling pioneers such as Louis Daguerre — his system involved nothing less hazardous than boiling mercury — and William Henry Fox Talbot, inventor of the negative.

Niépce's first snap required an eight-hour exposure. That's almost as long as some of the 'Supercar Classics' photographers take. Goddard celebrates the visit by immortalising Citroën with a pinhole camera, a technique that eschews a very expensive lens in favour of a piece of opaque paper punctured by one small hole. First attempt thwarted when devil-may-care local takes a riverside leak, unaware that he's in shot.

Volunteer as chauffeur for relaxed drive through grey afternoon. Blissful lack of traffic on Burgundy's rural roads conceals venerable four-cylinder's shortage of low down acceleration. Citroën experimented with six-cylinder engines, but lacked funds to produce them. That's one of the DS19's few shortcomings. In most other respects, space, comfort, ride, economy, aerodynamics, overall concept — it could be modern. A bit lurchy on corners, perhaps, but yesterday's dash vividly illustrated unexpected roadholding and handling qualities.

Map looks like a wine list, but Goddard's navigation steers us clear of temptation.

Brodie wonders if Bouze-les-Beaune is an invitation, rather than a placename. Despite the weather, spend a pleasant hour in Chateauneuf, a 12th Century village perched on a steep hill, high above the Autoroute du Soleil. Café in tiny square serves delicious apple-and-plum tart. Sermour-en-Auxois and cobble-stoned Noyers delight us en route to Chablis, but the day's highlight for the Citroënistes has been sight of a 2CV Sahara from the 1950s. Devised to defy desert, this Doox Chevoox sports four-wheel drive courtesy of front and rear engines.

Chablis is another nice little town. Hotel l'Etoile charges around £12 for a room, serves a fair five-course dinner for about £14, and provides ample opportunities to sample local lubricants. Grapes for top-ranking grand cru wines are limited to vineyards covering only 250 acres, on gentle slopes to east and north of Chablis. »

Blissful lack of traffic on Burgundy's rural roads conceals venerable four-cylinder's shortage of low down acceleration. Citroën experimented with six-cylinder engines, but lacked funds to produce them. That's one of the DS19's few shortcomings

Parked on the side of the
Saône river

Garé de long de la Saône

Local Citroën dealer
entrance

—

Brodie advertising Citroën to
the Parisians!

—

Martyn taking pinhole
photos on the quay at
Chalon-sur-Saône

Entrée de concessionnaire
Citroën

—

Brodie fait le publicite pour
Citroën aux Parisiens!

—

Martyn prenant photo
sténopé sur le quai à
Chalon-sur-Saône

*Who said these
skinny little
buggers don't grip
in the wet?*

Sunday

"Who said these skinny little buggers
don't grip in the wet?" Brodie challenged,
rhetorically, as the DS sped in the general
direction of Paris. Rain was pelting down
hard enough for prudent citizens to be
noting the ark-building instructions in
the sixth chapter of Genesis. Stop for
lunch in Fontainebleau, where half the
population of Japan is visiting the former
royal palace, most of which dates from
the 16th Century. The town's a tourist
trap, of course, but despite that we get an
acceptable three-course lunch for £5.50
a head.

The rain stops. On to bustling Paris by
mid-afternoon. Brodie commemorates
what may well be GBL 666C's first visit
to its spiritual home by lapping the Arc de
Triomphe at a speed worthy of Alain Prost
with Senna in his sights. Drive down the
Avenue des Champs-Élysées, noting such
quintessentially French establishments as

McDonald's and Burger King, then check
into Hotel de Calais, a 60 second saunter
from the Place Vendôme. This is another
old-style hotel — ornate brass bedsteads,
antique chairs trimmed with red velvet,
marble fireplaces. Around £50 is probably
not unreasonable for a room right in the
heart of one of the world's most beautiful
and vibrant cities.

Monsieur Morrow and friend join us for
dinner at Le Procope in the Rue Ancienne
Comédie. The other guest, Jean Blondeau,
is in the same line of business as Brodie.
Founded in 1686, Le Procope claims
to be the world's oldest café. The list of
famous patrons looked good even before
we arrived. Voltaire, Robespierre, Benjamin
Franklin, Napoleon... Hilarious evening
ends with a bill that could be mistaken for
distance in inches from Paris to Peking.

Driving through a Chablis
vineyard

—

Llewellin inspecting Brodie's
wine choice

—

Parked outside the hotel on
arrival

Traverse d'un un vignoble de
Chablis

—

Llewellin veille la choix des
vins par Brodie

—

Stationné à l'extérieur de
l'hôtel en arrivant

Monday

Briefly visit Blondeau's establishment, packed with post-war Citroëns, then point trusty DS's snout towards Calais. Goddard drives, for the first time, and is no less impressed than I've been. He doesn't go quite fast enough to join the 100mph club, which welcomed Llewellin on a deserted stretch of autoroute near Orleans. Speedometer is commendably accurate.

Arrive at Calais Hoverport to be told that the return ticket is from Boulogne! This gives Goddard excuse for 10-10ths charge down coast road. Channel like a millpond, so Prince of Wales completes crossing in 33 minutes, then it's back to the reality of south-east England's traffic. The astonishing DS19 has covered 1309 miles at 29mpg. Verdict? In terms of futuristic technology, if not scalding performance, yesterday's big Citroën demands and deserves a place of honour among the world's most outstanding classic cars. ◨

Brodie & Llewellin route-
planning

—

Casino at Néris-les-Bains

—

Turning on the Champs-
Élysées

—

Parked outside the hotel

Brodie & Llewellin
planification d'itinéraire

—

Casino de Néris-les-Bains

—

Passant sur les Champs-
Élysées

—

Stationné à l'extérieur
de l'hôtel

FOOTNOTE

Purists, please, it is indeed a 1965 Slough-built DW, one of the last made there. This car was a very lucky find and a direct result of always following up on offers. I went to see it, did not look at the mileage, just made a quick appraisal and said "What a nice car, keep it for yourself". But he insisted, so I bought it and only on rolling it out of his garage did I realise what a lovely find it truly was. It did the whole of this trip, a long journey, beautifully, as alluded to in the text.

The wine we drank in the Casino photograph was Château Brane-Cantenac '78; the other one that night I have forgotten…

We had a miserable day photographing in the rain amongst the vineyards of Chablis, before retiring to the modest but pleasant hotel in the town centre as mentioned by Phil. After dinner there, and despite warnings from his doctor, Phil, who was still recovering from his first heart attack, dragged Martyn and me into the bar where we consumed a glass of wine before Martyn retired. Then there was just Phil and me and a pleasant non-English couple. The two of us quietly got slightly sozzled and start talking to them, eventually making a little gentle fun of them as perhaps only Brits will. In the end, I lost my nerve about his health, and dragged Phil, protesting, to his room in deference to his doctor's orders.

The Champs-Élysées photo took about twenty attempts to get right and raised my stress level considerably. You have to have nerves of steel in photo-shoots sometimes.

I'd also like to mention that not only was Mr Bardinon hospitable (and spoke excellent English, rendering Mr Morrow superfluous), but he was also gracious enough to consult me on the lunch wine choice from his cellar, and to search out the DS, complimenting me on its condition!

—

ANDREW BRODIE 2012

The Rotary Club Outing

An exploratory trip around Alsace in two unusual cars

Words by Paul Horrell
Pictures by Martyn Goddard

A long-distance old-car jaunt needs a rigid itinerary like a bar mitzvah needs a plate of bacon sandwiches

It's hard to decide whether Andrew Brodie, who fixes Citroëns for a living, has complete faith in the marque or is merely a fatalist. We are about to set off on a 1200 mile tour in his recently bought and largely untried GS Birotor — a Citroën so rare and so unique under the skin that it's unlikely to be recognised even in the garages of France — and his total stash of spares and tools for the journey consists of two second-hand spark plugs and a Swiss army knife.

For ages I've been keen to do this trip. A year ago, a few miles in Ronald 'Steady' Barker's NSU Ro80 made me keen to go further. As a kid, I travelled tens of thousands of miles in my parents' two flat-four GSs and have loved virtually all of the dozens of Citroëns I have driven since, for their looks, comfort, and originality of engineering. The Birotor is as far as the Citroën philosophy went before financial chill forced the firm beneath the smothering blanket of Peugeot.

A long-distance old-car jaunt needs a rigid itinerary like a bar mitzvah needs a plate of bacon sandwiches. Amid an anarchic crescendo of hitches, glitches, breakdowns and foul-ups, the best-laid plans tend to collapse to rubble. Better to admit your impotence in the face of fate, and plan on having no plans. We have a few tentative aims and a hotel booked near Calais, but the rest of the trip is made up as we go along.

Andrew Brodie, the GS and your scribe convene at photographer Martyn Goddard's place in north London on a grey Tuesday lunchtime in November 1990. Brodie drives first: it's his car and, naturally, we're so late that a certain aggressiveness of driving style is in order. I cower in the back.

We meet 'Steady' and the Ro80 in Dover, take the hovercraft to Calais and find ourselves pitched into the French rush

hour. No worries, as tonight we have beds booked in advance, a dozen miles down the road at Ardres in the hotel Le Relais. 'Steady' has been here before, and the warm welcome and good food confirm why he is happy to come back. Smiting the Visa card (who needs a common European currency when we've got the plastic?) to the tune of £170 checks us out of Le Relais. Not bad value: about 40 percent of that is for the four rooms, the rest meals and drink.

Pre-start oil dipping (neither car uses much) reveals some interesting things about the twin-rotor Wankel engines. The GS engine bay, its motor mounted transversely with a spare wheel on top, is frighteningly crowded, whereas in the longitudinal Ro80, there's room around the engine for its brilliant, natural simplicity to be apparent. 'Steady's' is a special Ro80 in that its engine has been modified by plasma welding the combustion chambers to overcome the dreaded problem of rotor-tip seal wear.

The cars share engine ancillaries: a big twin-choke Solex carb and what appear to be identical ignition systems. Their main engine castings are superficially different, but the Citroën engine has a plaque attached to the effect that it was built under licence from NSU.

In 1967, Citroën was partner with NSU in setting up a rotary engine-building company called Comotor in the town of Colmar, Alsace, which, we decide, seems an appropriate destination for this journey. Comotor was just part of a long saga of financial wrangling in which, among other proposals, the two firms nearly merged then didn't, and NSU was bought by VW because VW wanted NSU's K70 design.

Though it's now as rare as a profitable Sinclair C5 dealership, this Birotor was one of 840-odd originally built in 1974/75. Brodie, as he inspected his example at home before the trip, was amazed how little it has in common with the normal

Both cars in Riquewihr

Les deux voitures à Riquewihr

Outside the Carriage
Museum in Compiègne
—
Passing a 2CV in the Ro80
—
Barker and Horrell start
the day

En dehors du musée de
Carrosses à Compiègne
—
Dépassement d'une 2CV
dans la Ro80
—
Barker et Horrell
commencent leur journée

GS. Flared wheel-arches aren't the only sheetmetal differences; the whole of the front end and the floorpan differ, too. The engine, driving a semi-automatic three-speed gearbox, is transverse instead of longitudinal, the front brakes are moved outboard, and suspension, brakes, hubs and wheels are all beefed up, using CX and SM components in some places.

Brodie has a brochure; it seems all Birotors came in two-tone bronze. Its sales figures were a disaster, as it was a lot dearer than a GS yet looked little different, cost as much to fuel as an SM, and had the famous engine-seal unreliability problem.

In autumn 1974, Comotor halted engine production in the face of a stockpile and soon Citroën pulled the plug on the car. The next bit will make you weep. To avoid the costly need to hold stocks of spare parts, Citroën bought back the cars, and crushed them; only a handful slipped through the net. There are no spares. If we crash this one, we reduce the world population by a significant proportion.

The Ro80's engineers never quite solved the unreliability or consumption problems, but their car was built in a 10 year run from 1967, to total 37,204 units. The engine develops 115bhp (the GS is quoted at 107bhp) and is slung out into the car's

nose, driving, as in the GS, a semi-automatic two-pedal transmission behind it, with inboard disc brakes.

It's an arrangement that allows a low bonnet and vast cabin, and the Ro80 has an elegant fantasy of a body shape to capitalise on it, running from the long nose to the high boat-tail via a huge, double-curved windscreen that has S-shaped pillars. It's also very aerodynamic.

We head onto the Paris Autoroute for the 120 miles to Compiègne. The Ro80 is a good motorway car, even today. The engine hum is quiet and sweet and road noise, the bane of fat-tyred moderns, is near absent.

I can't think of a small-to-medium modern car that rides as well

The ride is marvellously soft, smothering all the irregularities of the most casually laid concrete motorway. The flat-floored interior is vastly roomy.

The Citroën is just as able to cruise fast, rides as well, and has seats that are as comfortable. In fact, I can't think of a small-to-medium modern car that rides as well. But the GS is a noisier car, through road roar and wind rush around the haphazardly-sealed side windows. Its exhaust noise intrudes more than the NSU's: the Ro80 produces a seamless hum whereas the GS's note has a definite texture to it.

Compiègne is a noble town, and its grandest civic buildings house, among other things, the Musée National de la Voiture et du Tourisme. We are here for carriages, not cars. Rows of them are crammed into a vast, dingy hall, from early mail coaches to the horse-drawn transport of the aristocracy. Also here are horse-drawn charabancs, an early Citroën half-track desert vehicle and a colossal 1885 Amédée Bollée steam mail coach. This rumbling monster has underpinnings that would match a small railway locomotive for weight, and is the size of a modern double-decker bus.

A photo-session in front of the museum allows me time to crawl under the cars. The Ro80 is standard German fare — lower wishbones, MacPherson struts and coil springs at the front, semi-trailing arms and coils behind. The suspension isn't set up like a German car's, though. It's far softer, and though well enough damped for even spirited cornering, it does tend to roll an astonishing amount in bends.

The GS has double wishbones at the front and trailing arms behind, all suspended and damped by self-levelling hydropneumatic high-pressure valves and spheres. Where the Ro80 has light power steering, the GS does without, and suffers for it at low speed. Unlike the Ro, float and roll are well contained.

Heading east along busy main roads, the cars and crew soon need fuel. The GS uses a 10 gallon shot of sans plomb (no valves, so no need for lead) every 190 miles or so, and the Ro80, though it has a bigger tank, has an identical thirst in our hands.

On down the road to Reims, a busy city under an impressive cathedral. In traffic as well as on the open road, the GS transmission is nicer than the Ro80's with which it shares principles but not components. In the GS, moving the gearlever towards neutral sends hydraulic fluid to disengage the clutch. Into the next gear in the three-speed cogbox (not an auto-style epicyclic), and the clutch is re-engaged, the torque converter smoothing the take-up and covering up the rotary engine's comparative lack of low-end torque and slight splutteriness on the over-run.

The Ro80 has an electropneumatic clutch that's disengaged as soon as you touch

At speed on the Autoroute

À vitesse sur l'autoroute

Ro80 in Kayserberg vineyard
—
More attention needed…
Late for hotel!

Ro80 dans une vignoble à
Kayserberg
—
Plus d'attention nécessaire
…. En retard pour notre
hôtel!

We decide to drive to Metz, which will surely have industrial-scale hotels that will check us in at any hour

the lever in any direction — even if you brush your knee past it at full throttle on the motorway, which can be scary. Also engagement isn't as smooth as in the GS.

The bonuses of a semi-auto transmission are manifold: it's almost as lazy as a full auto, offering a big spread of speeds in each gear and no clutch work in town, where you can stop in gear and let the torque converter slip. Yet you retain full control of downchanges for engine braking and avoid unnecessary mid-corner shifts. Also, downchanges are smoother than with a full auto because you can blip the throttle.

Our destination in Reims is the Philippe Charbonneaux museum of French cars. Charbonneaux designed the Renault 16 and 8, worked for Figoni, styled Delahaye's 235, the last Bugatti T101, and in an interlude with Chevrolet laid the firm foundations for the first Corvette. There

have been hundreds of fascinating one-offs in his career, too. He's in his office this afternoon, and is happy to show an unexpected English party around the collection of hundreds of odd and mainstream French makes. There's even a GS Birotor engine on show. Brodie, lunatic Citroën fan, goes into orbit.

We need to cover some more miles. France shuts early, the streets of its small towns eerily deserted by eight in the evening, their hotels unwilling to take in late arrivals. So we decide to drive to Metz, which will surely have industrial-scale hotels that will check us in at any hour.

Nearly there and the Ro80 splutters. In the dark rain, a plug change sees to it, but 'Steady' can be pleased he brought a plug spanner. We joke that if you take your car to Hypertronics, Brodie's well-regarded Citroën-fettling outfit in north London,

you'll have to remember to take along your own socket set.

To compensate for the mechanical glitch, Metz provides luck at the first town-centre hotel we try, the Foch, and though it doesn't have a restaurant, there's a perfectly serviceable one, Le Canari, next door. The chatty proprietor is keen to give her English language a run, and directs us to her uncle's vineyard in Alsace.

After another fuel-up, we're gone from Metz first thing in the morning. On truck-choked trunk routes as we head south-east, the Birotor is a useful thing: left-hand drive for a start, and possessed of handy overtaking push in its wide-ranging second gear. I like the architecture of its interior; the curvy facia is over-styled and about as solidly assembled as one of John Noakes's sticky-backed plastic-and-squeegee bottle creations, but at least it's unusual. The

Ro80's dashboard is efficient but drab.

Up into the Vosges, drizzly weather and roadworks have plastered the cars with grime. We find a jet-wash machine in a Citroën garage, and while I clean up, Brodie spends a happy quarter-hour rummaging among the dozens of rusting Citroën carcasses around the back. He returns jubilant, having stumbled upon a rare and (he claims) valuable species of DS hubcap. Baffled by Brodie's enthusiasm, the garage owner says he can keep it, gratis.

After all this time, we still haven't had a decent punt of these cars on bendy roads, so we divert up into a few deserted Cols. It's wet, but there's fun to be had.

Uphill in the GS, the engine winds happily around the rev dial, issuing just enough power but no surfeit when it's this steep. The steering is accurate, but much lower-geared than any power-assisted Citroën system. A certain amount of torque-steer is evident, but the steering wheel is so full of

messages that you can happily explore the modest limits of grip. When you reach the edge of the envelope, it's understeer always.

The Ro80 is slightly less friendly. Its greater bulk is only a small handicap to pressing-on along small roads, but the light, feel-less steering distances you from the action. Eventually I fathom its subtle messages, and enjoy things a lot. Coming down the more open 180 degree mountain bends, the Ro80 is happy to be thrown into what might nearly be called drifts.

The Ro80 has perfectly fine servo-ed all-disc brakes, but it's no Citroën: the Birotor's no-slop pedal has an absolutely progressive and confidence-inspiring action over a very short travel. I love Citroën brakes.

By now the NSU is misbehaving badly. Cleaning the plugs brings relief for ever-briefer periods. We struggle on to the Alsace vineyards near Colmar, and lose patience. It gradually becomes clear, as we fiddle and poke about, that the two cars »

Brodie and Barker changing
spark plugs, again

—

Citroën dealer mechanics
surprised by rare Birotor

Brodie et Barker remplacent
les bougies d'allumage -
encore

—

Mécanique concessionnaire
Citroën surpris par Birotor
rare

Parked below Hunawihr
church

—

Slipping through a nearby
vineyard

Garé en dessous de l'église

Se faufilant à travers un
vignoble proche

have identical ignition systems, which must be of comfort if you own a Birotor with a clapped-out distributor. We swop rotor arms and plugs between Citroën and NSU, but it's still a no-go Ro.

'Steady' then plays his joker. The night before he left home, he had pulled the ignition booster box from his spare car, and packed it just in case. Goddard and I look for photos in the Birotor while 'Steady' and Brodie go about the roadside repairs.

We're on the Route du Vin, at Ribeauvillé. All around are rolling hills covered with vineyards, autumn-brown now. The vines are planted in small adjoining areas at different orientations, making the landscape resemble a heavily patched pair of brown cord trousers.

Back with the NSU, there's a look of triumph. The spare black box (actually silver in colour) did the trick, and we drive a few more miles to Ammerschwihr, to the cellars of the uncle of our Metz restaurateur. All the villages are dotted with cellars offering their own dry, fruity wines from Gewürztraminer, Muscat and Riesling grapes, plus the late-harvested, sweeter Vendage Tardives wine.

Along one of the cobbled streets beneath Kaysersberg's imposing fort we find a hotel. Before dinner, wine-lover Brodie realises we're only a hop away from Riquewihr, home of the famed house of Hugel's wines. We go sample its wares, and return with the GS's big boot clinking.

Flushed with success, Brodie, veteran of several Ecurie Supercar Classics French Citroën sorties, knows the psychological value of a celebratory meal. Besides, we missed lunch today. He selects the Chambard, a restaurant whose silver and starched linen are a notch or two upmarket for our oil-stained jeans, but which welcomes us happily. And provides superb food.

We go sample its wares, and return with the GS's big boot clinking

GS and a local 2CV

—

In a Riquewihr gateway leading to old town

GS et une 2CV

—

Porte d'entrée de la vieille ville à Riquewihr

Next day, we take advantage of the fact that Strasbourg and Calais are joined by direct Autoroute. A steady 90mph is easy, rolling along in thin traffic, crossing the giant agricultural north of France.

I'm driving the Ro80 when there's a tap-tap-rattle from behind that starts out as one of those noises you just can't ignore, and soon turns into one that you absolutely won't. Pulling over reveals the silencer dragging on the ground. It's heavy indeed, so I lever it back up into place with a marker post uprooted from the verge while Brodie and Barker wrestle successfully with its mounts. Goddard photographs the six legs poking from under the car, and keeps a lookout for those nice friendly Gendarmes.

On our way again, and still in time to catch the hovercraft, confirmed Citroëniste Brodie admits he'd rather have the NSU. I'd agree, but it's close. The glorious Ro80 is so complete, because it was designed around that engine. The GS is more agile but less refined, and that's a slight waste of the engine's qualities. A three-rotor CX? Yes, please. ◼

Ro80 in vineyard

—

Le Relais Hotel in Ardes

—

Replacing the notorious
black box

Ro80 dans le vignoble

—

Le Relais Hôtel à Ardes

—

Remplacement de la
boîte noire d'allumage
électronique

FOOTNOTE

The Compiègne coach museum contains the most amazing array of age-blackened leviathans. When we arrived in Alsace, always keen to make sure that the team got in a little fine dining, I arranged dinner at a nearby Michelin two-star restaurant.

"You wanted to come here; you choose and pay for the wine" they all cry. Exhausted, I survey the wine list and find a '76 Petits Grains Nobles Riesling at a mere 1000FF. Rather more tired than I realise, I miscalculate and divide by 100FF to the Pound, rather than 10, thinking it quite reasonable. They like it of course and demand a second bottle, also rapidly dispatched.

Yes, I did have to pay up on my own with no offers of assistance. The rest of the bill, though reasonable, shocked poor Steady who, as an important Motoring Journalist, normally never had to pay for food on trips.

We did indeed visit the sales room of the restaurant proprietor's uncle, deep in a cellar in an Alsace town. We were made welcome, and naturally were obliged to buy a few bottles.

Amusingly, the "unproven" Birotor completed the whole journey without a murmur, while we were often attending to the Ro80, highly stressfully, at night in the rain, and late for the not-yet arranged hotel. Always prepare!

Fortunately I had my trusty 1959 Civil Defence (CD, or "seedy") greatcoat with me to lie atop on the road while under Steady's car in the photo on the credits page. I still have it, though sadly the Birotor is gone to a better home.

Paul Horrell was also a Citroën GS fan and he bought a GSX3 just after this. I remember that he had to be gently eased into our style of travel, but no doubt he will demur... the Riesling helped.

—

ANDREW BRODIE 2012

Long Road Home

Four times a competitor in the Monte Carlo Rally and freshly restored in London, this Citroën 15-Six returned to its south of France home over the Rally's famous mountain roads with Phil Llewellin at the wheel

Words by Phil Llewellin
Pictures by Martyn Goddard

In broad terms, car design had
changed very little since the turn of the
century before the first Traction Avant
was launched

A glance at the Michelin Atlas Routier France confirmed that the road into the majestic Chartreuse mountains — our long journey's first major challenge — was liberally laced with hairpins and climbed almost 3000ft in eight or nine miles to reach the Col du Granier, high above Chambery. The ascent was tough enough to make a modern car work hard. We were about to tackle it in nothing more powerful or fleet-footed than a 42-year-old Citroën 15-Six, so the time had come to cross fingers, whisper a prayer and mutter encouragement while trying not to think about the radiator boiling, the clutch slipping and the oil pressure falling.

This was no jaunt in a car owned by one of the Citroën's three occupants. The big, black saloon — a rare version of the epochal Traction Avant whose debut in 1934 marked the birth of the modern car — was being returned to its lady owner, Margaret Ritson, following restoration in London. Mrs Ritson lives in Roquebrune Cap Martin, little more than a crankshafts's throw from Monte Carlo. It was there her husband bought the 15-Six in 1950. Fitted with three Solex carburettors, which were later removed, it contested the Monte Rally in 1951, 1952, 1953 and 1954, finishing as high as seventh.

Nothing if not a devoted Citroëniste — she owns four of the marque's classics — the lady agreed with Andrew Brodie when he suggested that running the 15-Six on Monte Carlo Rally roads in the Chartreuse and Vercors mountains would add a dash of spice to the delivery drive. Brodie's company had undertaken some of the restoration work. His credentials as a first-class travelling companion had been established during previous forays to France in a 1973 Citroën SM and a 1965 DS19. They range from a robust sense of humour to membership of the International Wine and Food Society.

As in the past, the trio was completed by Martyn Goddard. He has been known to rattle off a few rolls of Kodachrome when not rallying his Austin A40, posing in his big Healey, or pleading poverty while trying to sell me his immaculate SM.

Citroën's reputation for advanced technology made it appropriate to eschew the traditional ferry in favour of a first taste of Hoverspeed's sci-fi SeaCat. Designed to carry 80 vehicles and 450 passengers, the world's biggest catamaran whisked us from Folkestone to Boulogne in only 45 quiet, comfortable minutes. This was long enough for me to run through a few facts about the Citroën before taking the wheel for the first time.

In broad terms, car design had changed very little since the turn of the century before the first Traction Avant was launched. The traditional recipe's main ingredients were almost invariably rear-wheel drive and a separate chassis whose beam axles and leaf springs would not have puzzled a medieval wainwright. Citroën's newcomer, one of the few truly great cars, cast convention aside by featuring front-wheel drive, unitary construction and independent front suspension with wish-bones and torsion bars. The low-slung Traction was futuristic enough to remain in production until 1957. About 750,000 were built.

Known as the 15-Six in France, but the Six in Britain, the stretched version of the 1.9 litre, four-cylinder Traction was announced in 1938. Sixteen feet long, almost six wide and an inch over five high, this spacious saloon had a 2.8 litre engine. Fed by a single twin-choke Solex, the straight-six lived up to its truck-like appearance by developing only 76bhp at 3800rpm.

Although sprinkled with a few adverse comments, most of which ring true today, press reactions in general were very favourable. Tested by 'The Motor' in 1949, when it cost a few pence under £1087,

Driving towards Paris

En route vers Paris

Citroën's solution to the problems posed by French roads, which used to be notoriously rough, combined very efficient suspension with an exceptionally long wheelbase

the big Citroën reached 60mph in 19.4 seconds, sailed on to a record a top speed of 82mph and averaged 19.1mpg on the dish-water that passed for petrol in the early post-war years.

"A quite exceptional car" and "one of those rare cars that improve on one's best time for a familiar journey" are typical of comments in The 'Autocar' test, which appeared a month later and featured the same car.

Having admired these old Citroëns for as long as I can remember, I was fully prepared for an almighty letdown when Brodie vacated the driver's seat. By far the most important fact to remember was that the three-speed gearbox's lever, which protrudes from the centre of the dashboard, and is almost six feet from the actual cogs, has shift

positions quite unlike those of a modern car. If you think in terms of the four forward gears in a conventional H-shaped layout, Citroën's first is where you would expect fourth to be. Taking it from there, second is first, third is second and reverse is third.

This may sound complicated, but the risk of getting it wrong is almost eliminated by the slow, precise shift characteristics. The conveniently angled lever glides easily from slot to slot, helped by a discreet blip of throttle when changing down.

Cruising with ever-increasing confidence along the old, tree-lined roads of northern France, heading for an overnight stop north of Paris, soon made it clear that flexibility is the long-stroke engine's greatest asset. Although the 2.8 litre's power output is very

low by today's standards, and was described as modest even when the 15-Six was new, there's no need to apologise for 138lb-ft of torque at 2000rpm.

The ride had been praised long before we dropped anchor at La Ferme de Vaux in Creil, between Beauvais and Chantilly. Citroën's solution to the problems posed by French roads, which used to be notoriously rough, combined very efficient suspension with an exceptionally long wheelbase. On the other side of the balance sheet, nobody volunteered to juggle the 15-Six into a tight parking slot after we unloaded our bags. The rack-and-pinion steering is superb on the open road, but at very low speeds it demands the mindless muscles of a sumo wrestler on steroids and happy pills.

La Ferme de Vaux, which incorporates a 12th Century chapel, served an excellent six-course dinner for the equivalent of about £17.50. We might have been tempted to end the day by sorting out the world's problems over a cognac or two, but had to be on the road before dawn. Brodie's master plan called for us to be near Grenoble, about 400 miles away, by the end of the next day.

But the first priority was a brief meeting with a Citroën fettler in Paris, where these classy cars were built. It would have been appropriate to meet Brodie's pal somewhere on the Quai André Citroën, but practical considerations dictated snapping the 15-Six with Notre Dame in the background, then chatting over coffee and croissants in the Gare du Lyon. I have long been convinced that failing to eat a proper breakfast accounts for every French military disaster since Crécy in 1346.

Although the Traction appeared more than two decades before France had motorways, its ability to cruise all day at about 70mph and 3500rpm is a reminder that this has been a land of long, gently undulating straights since Roman times. Families enjoying a warm, lazy Sunday smiled, cheered and clapped as the long-striding, smooth-riding saloon swept southward on Michelin radials that no self respecting modern kid would consider wide enough for his bicycle.

Attracting the right sort of attention wasn't the only reason for feeling good as the Citroën reeled in the miles. Seats trimmed with a velvet cloth emphasised the interior's almost limousine-like proportions. Relaxing in the rear compartment, this six-footer had about 17 inches of space between his knees and the back of the driver's seat.

Brodie, Goddard and Llewellin are as cheerful a trio as you could hope to meet in a day's march, but I always set a few minutes aside to consider the less

comforting aspects of any classic car's design. As we neared the snow-capped Chartreuse mountains, where the Col de Granier's hairpins and gradients awaited us, I jotted down a note about yesterday's drum brakes being no match for today's discs in terms of stopping power and resistance to fade. The metal dashboard, and the ice-pick of a handbrake that lurks beneath it, could have been designed to rip flesh and cleave bones in the event of an accident.

We brimmed the 15 gallon tank in Chambery, having averaged 19.2mpg since leaving London, then pointed the burnished nose at the mountains it had first sniffed in 1951. Contrary to my expectations, if not those of my loyal Citroëniste companions, the old timer soared up the Col du Granier with all the grace of a great bird riding on thermals. Visions of being reduced to a first-gear crawl were replaced by the torque-y engine's ability to slog along in second and top. By the end of the afternoon, when the 15-Six had established itself as just about the most satisfactory pre-1960 saloon I've ever driven, I was complaining about being baulked by modern machinery.

André Gaudillere runs the Auberge de l'Echaillon in St. Quentin-sur-Isere. A few miles downstream, cliffs rise in steepling splendour across the valley from the mountains of Chartreuse. He greeted the unexpected guests with gasps of delight, because his father had owned a six-cylinder Traction in days of yore.

Next morning, the orange juice, coffee and croissants were accompanied by a French copy of the late Andrew Whyte's 'Cadillac' in the 'Great Marques' series from Octopus Books. Monsieur Gaudillere's dream is to own a classic, over-the-top Eldorado with fins the length of a high-kicking chorus girl's legs.

As expected, after the previous afternoon's doughty performance, the Citroën »

By the Seine at Notre Dame

A cote de la Seine à Notre Dame

The ascent was tough enough to make a modern car work hard

912

Granier
164 m

Topping the Col du Granier

Au sommet de la Col du Granier

was not in the least daunted by a long day on mountain roads. Having started the journey laden with all manner of assumptions about how such an old front-wheel-drive car would perform, I was constantly surprised by the absence of strong understeer and the tenacity of those skinny Michelins. Knowing the 2CV, I was equally delighted to discover that big brother's comfortable ride had not been achieved by making the suspension soft enough for jokes about grazed elbows to be appropriate. There's remarkably little roll, which is just as well in view of the split-bench front seat's lack of lateral support.

By mid-morning we could understand why Richard Binns, who used to navigate rally

We were reminded that big, swift Citroëns were favoured by the Resistance and the Gestapo

Going down the Col du Bourne
—
Climbing a Col towards Vercors
—
Vercors 1944 Resistance Fighters memorial

La descente du Col du Bourne
—
Grimpant le Col du Vercors
—
Mémorial de la résistance de 1944 à Vercors

cars during the sport's golden age, pin-points the Vercors as one of his favourite parts of France. Binns has been visiting the country for more than 30 years, and writing highly commended guidebooks about it since 1980.

We explored the dramatic Gorges de la Bourne — cliffs overhang the complete width of the road in places — before cruising the big Traction through a lovely landscape where vast ramparts of naked rock, climbing to more than 7000ft, overlook Alpine meadows stippled with the brightness of wild flowers. But a roadside memorial in the village of St. Julian-en-Vercors was one of many reminders that this natural fortress was anything

but peaceful in 1944, when the 'Secret Army' defied the German troops who had occupied France since 1940. They hoisted the French flag and declared the Vercors to be a free republic, but were slaughtered.

The greatest symbol of suffering is the cemetery and memorial at Vassieux-en-Vercors, a village which was totally destroyed when German gliders swooped down on 21st July 1944. The victims of the attack were aged from 18 months to 91 years. We were reminded that big, swift Citroëns were favoured by the Resistance and the Gestapo — the brutal secret police — during the long, dark years before D-Day heralded Germany's defeat.

We lingered over a sun-blessed alfresco lunch by the river in Chatillon-en-Diois, then headed for Gap and the Route Napoleon. Why did Brodie call a halt when he spotted a small Citroën garage in the middle of nowhere? Because the need to grease the 15-Six's driveshafts and several other components every 600 miles is a reminder that very frequent service intervals were taken for granted in the Traction's day.

Castellane is a pleasant little town on the road up which Napoleon marched in 1815, en route from exile in Elba to his fateful clash with the Duke of Wellington at Waterloo. Clustered round a square, it was a good a place as any for our last night amid the mountains that become increasingly impressive as France begins to rub shoulders with Italy. Locals smiled and pointed as we did a slow circuit of the square before deciding to try the Auberge

Bon Accueil. This was a good move, because the bill worked out at only £25 per head for dinner, bed and breakfast, plus a shared bottle of red wine.

A bed was about the only feature that my room had in common with a suite at the Hotel Negresco in Nice or the Hotel de Paris in Monte Carlo, neither of which was on the agenda for this trip, but it was perfectly adequate in relation to the price charged. Standards vary a lot in France, of course, but this journey was another reminder that eating and sleeping costs much less there than here. Dick Turpin should be the British hotel business's patron saint.

Margaret Ritson's Citroën SM, DS23 and H-type van — the one whose corrugated panels are as quintessentially French as snails in garlic butter — were lined up to greet us when we reached Roquebrune Cap Martin.

Arriving ahead of schedule was a tribute to the sterling qualities of a car that may well have more than 150,000 miles to its credit.

Among those mustered to welcome the 15-Six home were Ian Walker and Gerry Burgess, who was winner of the 1959 RAC Rally. Ian's exploits include driving the first Lotus Elite ever to contest a race. He won. Ian recalled doing the Monte Carlo Rally in a 7.0 litre Ford Falcon driven by Graham Hill. He said; "We had wheelspin in the dry, so you can imagine what it was like on ice!"

Listening to his anecdotes made us all the more grateful for having crossed the same mountains in good weather, driving a car as safe and civilised as the Citroën 15-Six. My admiration for the Traction Avant concept, and for the way it has stood the stern test of time, had increased with every turn of the wheels. ▨

A mid-journey grease
—

Driving through an Alpes
Maritimes village
—

On a side track by the Route
Napoleon

Graissage en Route
—

Conduire à travers un village
des Alpes Maritimes
—

Sur une petite route par la
Route Napoléon

Village of Gréolières
—
Mrs Ritson's fleet, all bought
from new except the Traction
which was her husband's
from new
—
Overlooking Monte Carlo

Village de Gréolières
—
La collection de Mme
Ritsons - tous acheté de
nouveau, sauf la Traction qui
appartenait de nouveau a
son mari
—
Au-dessus de Monte Carlo

Brodie at work above Monte
Carlo

—

Dashboard with centre
gearlever

—

Llewellin at lunch

—

1952 Monte Carlo Rally
start picture with routemap
we used

Brodie au travail au-dessus
de Monte Carlo

—

Tableau de bord avec
changement de vitesse au
centre

—

Llewellin au déjeuner

—

Image du début du Rallye de
Monte Carlo de 1952 avec
la carte de route que nous
avons utilisé

FOOTNOTE

Unusually, in deference to my wonderful friend and Traction owner Margaret Ritson, we cheated a little and put her Traction on the railway from Paris to Lyon, while ourselves staging in the Saab 2.0 Turbo that was our chase and return journey transport. I had fun over the Cols, with the Traction going like a TGV in its ideal second gear and easily keeping up with the flat-out Saab on the steep twisty roads.

Margaret, of course, greeted us on arrival with champagne and blinis on her spectacular patio overlooking Monaco, as she was wont to do with any visitor. How special it made us all feel.

I remember the scene of the Traction above Monaco, and watching as Martyn composed the shot, and then walked ten paces away from the camera to remove a barely visible cigarette end that I certainly had not noticed. No Photoshop in those days.

Just to make the point that these trips were not all relaxing and imbibing, our departure from Margaret's was a very early start indeed as we had a museum photo-shoot arranged west of Tours for the same day. I did a fair bit of driving with the cruise control set to just slow enough not to get nicked and avoided the brake pedal at all costs. Martyn and Phil both then rightly told me off severely for speeding up when we left the Autoroute!

Yes, we got the shoot done. An early start was actually normal. You cannot rely on getting a second chance, so seize the moment and work, work, work 'till you have it in the can is the only way.
—

ANDREW BRODIE 2012

Continental Drifter

How does the once-futuristic Citroën DS measure up
as a late-Nineties Continental tourer?
Phil Llewellin lopes though France and the Low Countries in a DS23 Pallas

Words by Phil Llewellin
Pictures by Martyn Goddard

I was driving a prizewinning Citroën DS23 Pallas EFI that first turned a wheel in 1973

In the Calais hinterland

L'arrière-pays de Calais

Stygean night arrived early as rain torrented down from steeples skimming clouds black and menacing enough to conjure up thoughts of Armageddon. Ferocious weather combined with roadworks, accidents, bewildering signs and heavy traffic to shatter our schedule, adding three hours to what was always going to be a long day. But I was far less red-eyed and white-knuckled than you might expect when we dropped anchor near France's frontier with Belgium and rewarded ourselves with a few of the phenomenally strong beers brewed by monks in nearby Chimay.

An expensive modern car would have earned high praise for coping so admirably. In fact, I was driving a prize-winning Citroën DS23 Pallas EFI that first turned a wheel in 1973 and has been owned by Andrew Brodie since 1978. The big, shark-nosed, front-wheel-drive car's pace and poise in such testing conditions stood out as all the more remarkable when we reminded ourselves that this model, the last of the line, was developed from the futuristic DS19, which made its sensational debut at the Paris Motor Show way, way back in 1955.

The fact that Andrew Brodie Engineering's chief executive officer, sales director, PR manager and spannerman-in-chief didn't hesitate to make his beloved 'Déesse' available for a five-day, 1200 mile journey as winter was sinking its fangs into Europe endorsed Andrew's status as one of the good guys. As well as being a passionate, professional Citroëniste, he laughs a lot and has a serious connoisseur's grasp of food and fermented grape juice. This story could be subtitled 'The Three Musketeers ride yet again', because Brodie, yours truly and photographer Martyn Goddard had ventured abroad together before, in a Citroën Big Six, a low-mileage DS19 and a seriously swift SM. Having fun with like-minded friends was but one of several good reasons for this expedition to France, Belgium and the Netherlands. Aside from that, I wanted to gather material for future 'Classic Cars' features — watch this space — while looking at how the DS23 measured up as an alternative to a modern saloon. There was plenty of time to run through the specification, because what had been in the script as an overnight crossing from Portsmouth to Le Havre ended up in a delay of several hours as Hurricane Lili's furiously lashing tail forced our ferry to seek shelter off the Isle of Wight.

Early versions of the DS relied on a 1.9 litre engine inherited from Citroën's pre-war Traction Avant, which is widely hailed as the first "modern" car. Launched in 1972, the DS23 EFI was powered by a four-cylinder, 2.3 litre motor with five main bearings, electronic Bosch fuel injection and an aluminium head bolted to its cast-iron block. Key numbers included 141bhp at 5500rpm and 148lb-ft of torque at 4000rpm. The all-mod-cons Pallas version tested by 'Motor' in 1973 reached 60mph in 10.4 seconds — quicker than such rivals as the Mercedes 220, NSU Ro80 and Ford Granada 3000 — and ran out of steam within a whisker of 120mph, while averaging 18.6mpg. Despite plenty of brisk driving, we were to record 23.4mpg. The fully equipped French flagship cost £2839 when Jaguar's XJ6 was £3071 and Rover's 3500S was listed at £2207. Other aspects of the DS's unique design had been discussed during the stormy drive from London to Portsmouth. At a time when many rivals still relied on primitive leaf springs, little changed since the horse-and-cart era, Citroën's aerodynamically light-years-ahead roadgoing spacecraft had a fully independent self-levelling system, with the capability for selectable-from-the-driver's-seat boosting upward for wheel changing or stream fording.

The high-pressure hydraulics that operate the suspension also power the brakes,

Phil at speed in the DS

—

On Route Nationale in France
reading up about the Grand
Prix circuits and history

Phil à vitesse dans la DS

—

Sur la route nationale en
France, en étudiant l'histoire
et les circuits du Grand Prix

steering and a clutchless gearchange, which works by flicking a pencil-sized lever located within a finger's stretch of the single-spoke steering wheel. Cibié headlights powerful enough to ignite haystacks in France while driving through Italy swivel in unison with the front wheels; the outer ones are kept level by linkage to the anti-roll bar. All this good stuff is wrapped up in about the most distinctive body ever built in significant numbers. No wonder Brodie has scant regard for modern cars: "Bloody washing machines…"

Relaxing in the spacious rear accommodation as Andrew carved a swift, purposeful path through rush-hour London traffic, I appreciated the hydropneumatic suspension's ability to cope with all manner of road surfaces. I also noticed how much the Pallas pitched under hard acceleration and severe braking. This was a reminder that these soft-riding Citroëns are at their best when driven with attention to smoothness. We were far more concerned about how much P&O's 'Pride of Portsmouth' would pitch, roll and wallow during what was left of the night — but the worst of the storm had passed by the time we found our cabin, down amid rattling chains, deep enough to hear submariners snoring.

The plan was to visit a few racetracks, old and new, while zigging and zagging in the general direction of the Netherlands. But most of the morning had slipped away by the time we jumped ship. Days being short in winter, we were under pressure. And it was raining.

Working the wipers wasn't a problem but the DS's minor controls and instruments win no prizes for ergonomic efficiency, giving the impression of having been designed by flinging darts at a dashboard while blindfolded. Even starting was a puzzle until I realised that what you do, having turned the ignition key, is push the little gearlever to the left. What appears to be the clutch is the parking brake; releasing that was another teaser until Brodie pointed out a knob under the steering column.

Rouen, Dieppe, Amiens and Péronne were ticked off the bingo card before we plugged into the autoroute network for a slog across the Belgian frontier to Liége. Long before that, visions of a three-hour gourmet lunch had given way to the reality of an on-the-move snack. Fortunately Brodie, the chairman of the Food and Wine Society's London branch, had been prudent enough to leave home with chicken sandwiches big enough for King Kong.

Admiration for the Pallas increased with every roll of the wheels. On the road, it's important to remember that Citroën's answer to the conventional brake pedal is a black rubber mushroom. Instead of demanding an inch or three of movement, it reacts to the sort of pressure that a small butterfly's wing might exert. You get the impression that a fraction of the muscle needed to bully most old cars into shedding speed would make the DS23 perform more somersaults than an Olympic gymnast with ants in her leotard.

As expected, this tribute to innovative French engineering was in its element wafting down long, tree-lined straights and sweeping majestically through fast bends, its suspension insulating us from ruts, potholes, ridges and ripples. We were treated to a vivid illustration of what understeer is all about, however, when the pitch-black night suddenly hit us with a 'Stop' sign inches before a junction where a sharp corner had to be negotiated. Brodie's control of the big car on grass was impressive…

Needing to reach Liége in time for a meal was our excuse for storming along one deserted stretch of motorway at over 100mph. While appreciating the ability to maintain that speed up hill and down dale, we had to admit that significantly lower noise levels made 80-85mph much more enjoyable. The short-stroke engine sounded gruff when working hard and the big, frameless windows were sucked away from their seals.

These were reminders that early versions of Citroën's post-war masterpiece were over 30mph slower than the DS23 EFI. In a perfect world funds would have been available to eliminate such niggles, but Citroën was adrift in stormy waters as the DS neared the end of its long life, and would have sunk with all hands had Peugeot not provided a lifeboat.

Liége's highlights included an educational but unintentional tour of the red-light district before we found a hotel. Unfortunately, its prices were not so much steep as vertical. Our attempts to balance the books by choosing from the cheapest table d'hôte menu were thwarted when Brodie blew £30 on a bottle of claret. He needed soothing, because a stone flung up while passing a truck had smashed one of the car's huge glass headlight shields.

That broken headlight glass
—
Trademark chevrons
—
Roof-mounted turn signal
—
Boot badges

La lentille cassée
—
Les chevrons de la Citroën
—
Les Clignotants montés sur le toit
—
Insignes sur le coffre

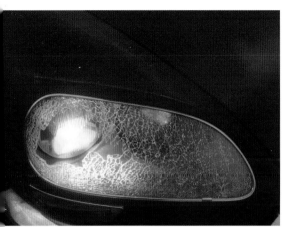  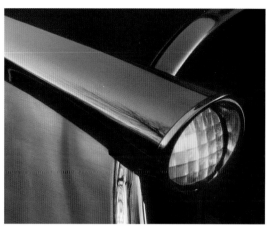 

We were treated to a vivid illustration of what understeer is all about, however, when the pitch-black night suddenly hit us with a 'Stop' sign inches before a junction

Parked in Stavelot
—
French graveyard headstone
of Wilfred Owen, WW1 poet

Stationné à Stavelot
—
Wilfred Owen, poète WW1,
une plaque commémorative
dans le cimetière français

Highlights of the following day included driving round those sections of the terrific Spa-Francorchamps circuit that coincide with public roads, then a photography pause in the very pleasant little town of Stavelot

Highlights of the following day included driving round those sections of the terrific Spa-Francorchamps circuit that coincide with public roads, then a photography pause in the very pleasant little town of Stavelot. The Musée du Circuit was, alas, closed for the winter. From there we looped north-westward into the Netherlands on what proved to be a very rewarding quest for fascinating cars and characters. In the evening, there was something almost surreal about eating an excellent Chinese meal in the land of clogs and windmills.

We gave thanks for hosts whose English was flawless, because my few talents do not include understanding Dutch spoken with a Cantonese accent. This would have been almost as difficult as working out what's what under the DS's bonnet, where enough pipes, hoses, wires, drums, canisters and contra-rotating throstle sprockets to equip a mad professor's laboratory make even so

much as establishing the location of the engine a task worthy of Sherlock Holmes. As noodles were nurdled, references to mind-boggling complexity were swept aside by Brodie's talk of proven reliability. The astonishing DS was not a flash-in-the-pan car, he insisted. It was the inheritor of the reputation earned by the pioneering Traction Avant, which had stayed in production for 21 years. Citroën took 12,000 orders for the DS on the day of its debut, and almost 1,500,000 were sold between 1955 and 1975, when the sleek CX was unveiled as its successor.

If there had been any lingering doubts about the DS Pallas EFI's ability to cope with modern traffic in foul weather, they would have been eliminated during the slog described in the introduction to this story. Restricted rearward visibility was one of the few quibbles worth mentioning as we relaxed in the lakeside Auberge des

Étangs des Moines, between Reims and Mons. Next day we made for the ferry by way of Ors, where one of my heroes, Wilfred Owen, poet and soldier, was killed in November 1918, just before the guns fell silent on the Western Front. He was born within sight of the house that I lived in from 1947-65.

The gently undulating landscape of northern France is stippled with war cemeteries and place names that appear on many a regiment's battle honours. As the Citroën cruised along those quintessentially French roads, I gave silent thanks for being able to glide so swiftly and easily across land where previous generations of my countrymen trudged to their deaths through rain, sleet and mud. In more ways than one, the DS23 was as much a time machine as a Dan Dare spaceship on wheels. ◼

En route to Picardie GP
circuit
—
On Chimay GP circuit, note
broken headlight glass

En route vers le circuit
Picardie GP
—
Le circuit GP de Chimay,
remarquez le verre brisé

On the track at Spa, just past
Eau Rouge

Sur la piste de course ar Spa,
après Eau Rouge

Old cars in a barn behind
a unique Dutch museum/
car dealer
—
Dash detail
—
Overtaken by Citroen CX
in the Calais hinterland
—
Photo of Jim Clark on
rear shelf

Voitures anciennes dans une
grange derrière un musée
unique néerlandais combiné
avec une surface de vente
—
Détail du tableau de bord
—
Dépassée par Citroën CX
dans l'arrière-pays de Calais
—
Photo de Jim Clark sur le
plateau de voiture arrière

FOOTNOTE

The grass-manoeuvring in the text was actually an involuntary crossing of a small roundabout, right over the centre, entirely my fault of course, as I was going too fast to drive around when it suddenly appeared out of the dark and rain. I was so very lucky; I only got a little murmur from the back seat.

This trip was the only one where untoward incidents reduced our pleasure a little. I remain very particular that cars tested should be perfect; it is asking too much of people to write around faults. Though very tired having thrashed through the rain and dark, I was delegated to park the DS in the Liège hotel car park, and caught the bottom of a rear door on an unmarked hazard on the up ramp. Then the headlight fairing glass shattered, the only DS one I have lost on the road (though there are a lot of gravel lorries in Belgium so watch out!). Arranging photos so that neither defect showed badly in the results added to our difficulties with the weather, but of course Martyn as ever took it in his stride. Then we were away from the car looking at an abandoned race spectator stand only to have Martyn shout "look" as the DS rolled off backwards down a hill because the parking brake was not set firmly. It calmly slowed to a stop undamaged before I could reach it.

One night we left our hotel near Chimay to find our chosen restaurant. Again tired and in need of refreshment, we drove in circles for quite some distance trying in vain to find the restaurant before discovering to our amusement that it was in the basement of our hotel, which was built on the side of a hill. No GPS in those days. But we did get consolation from a very varied selection of the local Monastic beers afterwards in the bar...!
—

ANDREW BRODIE 2012

French Connection

*There's a French ancestor in the Quattroporte family tree,
and they have more in common than you might first imagine*

Words by Dale Drinnon
Pictures by Martyn Goddard

No wonder we've turned every head we passed since setting out from Martyn's place in London

S tanding at the bathroom mirror on Sunday morning, razor in hand, eyes a trifle bleary, and suddenly there's an almighty whoop! of revs from somewhere downstairs. First thought from wine-dulled brain: Good God, is there a Grand Prix on television? Surely I haven't slept that late, have I? Sounds like they're cranking up for the formation lap…

Then I remember that Martyn was getting up early to do some close-up photos; the mighty rip of racing engine I've just heard is him moving our 4-door Maserati premium luxury car across the driveway.

No wonder we've turned every head we passed since setting out from Martyn's place in London — and at five o'clock in the bloody AM, to boot; his neighbours must have been delighted. From inside the car, the noise is stirring but unobtrusive; outside it will stand your hair on end. And it isn't the volume that grabs you, the Quattroporte really isn't terribly loud, it's the tone and intensity. Somehow, the Ferrari engineers responsible for the latest rebirth of the famous 4P have managed to build a traditional Maser V8 with a healthy added dose of full-race V10: imagine shoving a microphone up the tail pipe of Michael Schumacher's F1 car, adding a little bass, and playing it back at "two" instead of "eleven".

Of course, this car would be a traffic-stopper on its Pininfarina looks alone; it's aggressive, elegant, and simple and there's just enough nostalgia to tell the world I Have History. In black-on-black with tinted windows, the effect is deliciously ominous, too, and even down here on the Côte d'Azur, where the latest big Merc draws about the same notice as a white van in an industrial estate, passers-by will wait in turns just to run their fingers over the Quattroporte's sexy, sculpted door handles.

Add some reflected glory from the original Quattroporte of the '60s and the ailing Fiat Empire's entry into the prestige super-saloon category would seem to have an early leg-up; nothing from Audi, BMW, Jaguar or anybody else can drop an envious jaw quite like the Trident. But to see how it rates as a working automobile, we've brought it to the south of France for a comparison with its long lost cousin, the Citroën SM.

At rest for lunch in Mons

Repos et déjeuner à Mons

What could be better than their own avant-garde chassis combined with the magic of a thoroughbred Italian engine?

Which isn't as far-fetched as you're thinking. You see, among the many owners of the Maserati name since the Brothers went belly-up in the '30s was none other than Citroën, 1968 to 1975. Like Ferrari when Fiat handed them the reins, Citroën decided this was the perfect opportunity to explore new market segments, to tap into a lucrative customer base outside their normal product range, and also like Ferrari, they saw their new link with Maserati as the perfect tool for the job. What could be better than their own avant-garde chassis combined with the magic of a thoroughbred Italian engine?

That's where the Citroën Série Maserati comes in, along with our travelling companion and Citroën expert, Andrew Brodie. Andrew specializes in these V6, quad-cam French techno-GTs, particularly in making them quicker, and one of his very best belongs to Michael Quinlan. Michael is an expatriate Brit who lives in Monte Carlo, loves interesting and unusual cars, and keeps an outstanding cellar. Hence the wine-dulled brain, hence the Côte d'Azur. Yes, it's a tough old life, isn't it?

Anyway, Michael bought this 1972 model in 1990 and drove it happily until about three years ago, when he finally decided it needed a touch more oomph and rang Andrew. It isn't an uncommon complaint; thumping great French taxes on engines over 2.7 litres held the Maserati engineers

down to only 2670cc and 170bhp, not a lot for a ton-and-a-half of Citroën that uses an engine-driven hydraulic pump to run the power steering, brakes and self-levelling suspension. Andrew's answer was the time-honoured hot-rodder's universal fix — drop in a bigger motor. In this case, it's the 3 litre edition of the same V6, the big-valve version exclusive to the Maserati Merak SS. That gives this SM a boost of 50 extra horsepower, and Andrew built it using all the lessons he's learned about keeping these once-finicky engines together under pressure.

But first, a few words about driving the beautiful, exciting new Quattroporte south along the wide, sweeping motorways of France: frankly, it was kind of a mixed lot. First of all, this was Bastille Day weekend, the busiest of the year for French traffic and French traffic cops, and there was absolutely no way to give the car its head. (Besides, the first rule of automotive journalism is "Don't smash the car until the photographs are done.")

Furthermore, for a vehicle that aspires toward state of the art, some things are rather behind the competition. The nav system/multi-function display, for example, is ponderously awkward (I never did figure out how to turn off the fecking radio) and if the navigator is wearing polarized sunglasses, the screen disappears. There is no all-wheel drive, no soft-close doors, the turning circle is a stately 40 feet, »

SM overtaking Quattroporte

La SM dépasse le Quattroporte

Quattroporte cornering hard

Quattroporte virages serrés

I was dying to see how the Citroën-Maserati's reputation as one of the great highway cars stood up against the far newer Ferrari-Maserati

ride quality around town is choppy, and the brake pedal has that squishy ABS feel.

The biggest puzzlement, though, is the 'DuoSelect' gearbox. (They call the active suspension 'Skyhook'. Go figure.) It's the only box offered, and it's a six-speed sequential manual that can be shifted F1 fashion with steering column paddles, or left to shift automatically via computer control. Upshifts are sluggish in manual mode; in automatic, they're glacial, and the system is easily confused in slow manoeuvring situations. To engage reverse, there's a tiny fiddly lever on the centre console to lift and pull, followed by an idiotic warning beeper that leaves you feeling like a lorry driver squaring up to the dock with a delivery of bananas.

On the other hand, when you get an opening the 4P is awesome for carving up an Autoroute, and any shifting you do out there is strictly for your own amusement.

With 400bhp on call, there isn't much you can't leave for dead merely by rolling on the throttle. The 'Skyhook' feels firmly planted and secure, and trundling along between the caravans through those interminable parts of French farmland that look like southern Indiana without the exotic charm, the front armrest refrigerator and the double-adjustable lumbar support are manna from heaven. Still, for eighty thousand quid, you'd think they could at least offer you the option of a nice 5-speed…

So when the close-ups were finished, the coffee downed and we hit the road for the mountain sections, I made sure I got the first stint in the SM. This would start out with motorway before jumping off for the climb into the hills, and I was dying to see how the Citroën-Maserati's reputation as one of the great highway cars stood up against the far newer Ferrari-Maserati.

The answer is: not bad at all, thank you, and with not many allowances for the age difference, either. In fact, three decades on, the SM still does some things better than most anything else going.

The key to the Citroën-Maserati is that it is first of all a Citroën, with the funky, functional mannerisms that implies. Yes, the mushroom brake pedal will throw you against the windscreen. Yes, the arse-end jumps in the air when the engine starts and the turn indicators don't self-cancel and the steering wheel always returns to centre position, even if you switch off the ignition. Running down the A8 from Nice at 100mph, though, the ride quality is better than a limo trip through the park, and a sudden lane change is, well, only another lane change. The combination of comfort and control from the legendary hydropneumatic suspension is phenomenal and the rear seat passengers have it just as

SM chasing Quattroporte

SM en poursuite du
Quattroporte

easy as the front — as long as they're not too tall. That roofline does slope down a bit.

Past Cannes, off the Autoroute and swinging around toward the village of Mons, the single-carriageway turns twisty and starts to rise. This is where a normal 2.7 litre would be getting breathless, and where Andrew's engine upgrade is worth its weight in gold. As I get more accustomed to two turns lock-to-lock and the surprisingly flat torque curve under that forest of Webers (suitably encouraged by Andrew in the passenger's seat, yelling "don't steer, don't steer, don't steer, STEER!" followed by "now floor it!"), it becomes increasingly obvious the long, wide Citroën can be hustled along the back roads far faster than you'd think. Plus, it has a wonderful, conventional 5-speed with a fantastic gated shifter. Hallelujah.

More photographs on the road along the way, a few shots against the backdrop of scenic Mons, and lunch in the village: fortunately, far enough off the main tourist routes to yet be relatively quiet and unmolested. Perhaps not so quiet, though, with the four of us waving hands through the air like Spitfire pilots after a dog-fight, replaying the morning's drive and debating each car's place in the ultimate scheme of things. At the end, I'm still not sure I know exactly what Maserati intends for you to have in exchange for 80 large, whereas the SM's Grand Touring message seems straight and to the point.

Back into the Maser, then, for the afternoon session, the last of the photographs, and

maybe a chance to stretch it out a tad on some open road. With that in mind, we jiggle up the goat-path D563 to the N85, a lovely smooth thoroughfare running along the ridges toward Grasse, which has today apparently attracted every estate car with an overloaded roof rack in the entire country. So much for that, might as well find a quiet track off to the side and finish the shoot with the car-to-car pictures. This involves Andrew leading in the SM, while Martyn snaps me driving down one of those bumpy Monte Carlo Rally roads about half a lane wider than the car with a bottomless drop-off opposite a sheer wall of rock. It's dull and nerve-wracking stuff, and it's a relief when they pull up at a wide spot and Martyn says, "That's all. See you back at the main road." Andrew whips the SM around and promptly zooms back down the mountain.

Naturally, it's only after they disappear that I discover I've got about twice too much car for this turnaround — I also have no idea where they're going, and my mobile is in their car. With the huge turning circle and the stupid joystick reverse, my three-point turn has eight points, and by the fifth, I am officially Over It. On the final ungainly, frustrating lurch that gets me pointed the right direction, I punch the button for manual shifting, hiss "Okay, yeah, what have you got?" and stomp my right foot to the floor. The next several miles are what you might call a life changing experience…

… And I think I know now what Maserati is offering for your 80 grand, and don't be fooled by that premium luxury crap, it's

only clever window dressing. Underneath it, the car is monumentally, shockingly fast, and an absolute 400 horsepower hooligan. Maybe a hooligan wearing a nice suit, but when you push, it's a hooligan nonetheless; the harder you drive, the better it likes it. On tight turns, you'd swear the car gets smaller, and no matter how narrow or rough the surface, you can place it like a kart. The harder you use the brakes, the firmer they feel; the shifting gets better the higher you wind, and on full-bore downshifts, the computer even throws in a glorious, arrogant throttle blip. It is a car to be driven, as they say, like you stole it, and that's something no other big 4-door understands, much less strives toward.

As for the computer screens, rear air con and the like, I think the designers considered all that just the price of admission to the category, things you have to have before anyone will take an expensive saloon seriously. The key to the Quattroporte is that it's first of all a Ferrari, the sole true survivor of a long line of Italian cars meant above all else to be driven. Screaming down a French mountainside at 7000rpms with the exhaust bouncing off the stone face, you realize that in their own different ways, the Quattroporte and the SM are just as unusual and marvellous as each other: cars made by and for people more concerned with their own opinions than consumer focus groups. Screw the on-board navigation system; I'll buy a map. ◆

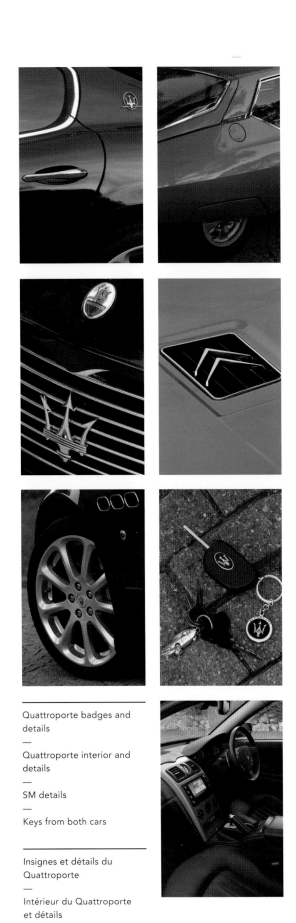

Quattroporte badges and details

—

Quattroporte interior and details

—

SM details

—

Keys from both cars

Insignes et détails du Quattroporte

—

Intérieur du Quattroporte et détails

—

Détails du SM

—

Clefs des deux voitures

FOOTNOTE

This trip and the next were intended to be a welcome reunion of the team, but very sadly Phil died suddenly and Dale Drinnon stepped in at short notice at Martyn's suggestion. I had made some of the arrangements but for once we were not using my own car.

We did get a lot of admiring stares; the Maserati Quattroporte was new, remains very pretty, and is fine for high speed Autoroute dashes. We got down to the Côte d' Azur in style.

The trip was memorable for the teeth-smashingly hard ride of the QP around London streets, and my catching Martyn's camera on a low wall. It was attached to the side of the QP for driving shots (I had a choice between being close to the wall or to the oncoming lorry, the camera temporarily forgotten in concern for the car. Quattroportes are not cheap). Martyn restrained himself… eventually. You really have to concentrate while doing these shots.

I was also tasked with manoeuvring the QP for a difficult multi-point turn in a rocky field by the side of the road. Quattroportes had then a reputation for burning clutches (electronically controlled) and indeed, I needed a gas mask on completion. The SM was just a delight in comparison — fast, fluid and comfortable.

—

ANDREW BRODIE 2012

Yesterday's Hero

A Red Wind rushing through the Alpes Maritimes

Words by Dale Drinnon
Pictures by Martyn Goddard

"Oh yes, it's gorgeous," said owner Michael Quinlan.
"That's one of the reasons I bought it…"

A mountain road inland from
the Côte d'Azur
—
Interior is classically Italian
—
The mark of the Trident

Une route de montagne en
partant de la Côte d'Azur
—
L'intérieur est classique Italienne
—
La marque du Trident

Okay, let's see now… Table of Contents… Lancia, Lotus — wait, here it is: Maserati. Maserati Bora, Maserati Ghibli, Maserati Mistral… nothing for Maserati Khamsin. Not a word. As far as the big, glossy 'World Supercars to Wet Yourself Over' type of coffee table publication is concerned, the Khamsin never existed. The DeLorean or the Porsche 924 might get some coverage, mind you, but not the Khamsin. You won't see it mentioned all that often in the enthusiast press, either. For a genuine 170mph Italian thoroughbred exotic, for the car that was the legendary Trident's last and arguably best traditional front-engined GT, the recognition it gets is decidedly underwhelming.

Tough to figure, and tougher still when I was standing contentedly alongside one, contemplating the exquisite shape in the soft early light of a Mediterranean summer morning, totally unable to find a bad line anywhere. "God," I sighed, with a tone perhaps slightly too evocative of the aforementioned book title, "it is a beautiful thing, isn't it?"

"Oh yes, it's gorgeous," said owner Michael Quinlan. "That's one of the reasons I bought it. That and the price; it just seemed like so much style and performance for the money." And the figure he quoted to me at that point, while not exactly pocket change, was a lot closer to new Japanese MPV than to classic Ferrari Daytona. Then he paused for a moment. "To be honest, though, I wasn't specifically looking for a Khamsin;

what originally attracted me was all the Citroën pieces."

Which rather strikes straight to the heart of the model's public profile dilemma. The Khamsin was a product of Maserati's brief stewardship by the French firm better known for daringly engineered saloons than for grand prix glory and, along with siblings Bora and Merak, it shares some of Citroën's fascinating and innovative but definitely non-Italian technologies. For a dyed-in-the-wool Citroën man like Michael, this is a positive attribute.

As you might recall, Michael is the British expatriate Monégasque who recently invited us to bring down the new Maserati Quattroporte and try it out through the breathtaking mountains of southern France against his lovely Citroën SM. "Actually,

I had been considering a Bora, but a couple of years ago I went to a Christie's auction and saw this, loved the combination of engineering and styling, and started bidding. As a point of interest it once belonged to Mike Oldfield, the fellow who did 'Tubular Bells'. Didn't seem to push up the final price, though…I guess it's been a long time since 'The Exorcist'."

But if the Khamsin is appreciated by progressives like Michael, it was not so well received by the cognoscenti of the 1970s — and still isn't. Total sales then were a third of its predecessor the Ghibli, a problem that was often attributed to the first oil crisis yet somehow didn't harm contemporary sales of the equally thirsty Ferrari Boxer, and in today's market the Ghibli is typically worth a 30 to 40 percent premium over a comparable Khamsin. If there is any surprise in this, however, it's only that anyone is surprised. Cars are bought with the heart as much as with the head, most emphatically so by those of us who love Italian cars, and from day one the model has been dogged by whispers that it's "not a real Maserati".

It's a shame, because in reality the Khamsin's bloodlines are fundamentally as pure as any other post-war Maser road car. Conceived at Bertone as the Ghibli's replacement, it debuted at the 1972 Torino Show and entered series production in '74, ironically just before Citroën and Maserati parted company. The designer was Marcello Gandini, whose other work includes the iconic Lamborghini Miura and Countach, the Alfa Montreal and the Lancia Stratos.

Unlike the mid-engined Bora and Merak, the first two cars introduced after Citroën's 1968 takeover, the Khamsin's layout is dead conventional: front-engined, rear-drive, long-bonnet Italian Grand Tourer. In physical dimensions and basic silhouette it is an almost identical twin to the Ghibli, and they share the same quad-cam,

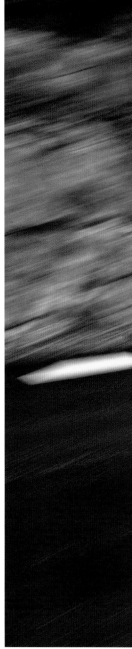

From day one the model has been dogged by whispers that it's "not a real Maserati"

Styling by Bertone, courtesy of
the great Marcello Gandini

Styling par Bertone, grâce à
Marcello Gandini

90 degree V8 engine design that goes all
the way back to the thundering Tipo 450S
sports racer of 1956.

In fact, direct visual evidence of Citroën
influence is pretty hard to find, even when
you're looking for it. Practically speaking,
Citroën approached the mechanical
relationship with Maserati as a mutually
beneficial technology exchange: from the
Italians, they got the neat little V6 that
went in the flagship SM coupé, and in
return Maserati got bits of their famous
hydraulic expertise.

For the Khamsin, this meant an engine-
powered pump to assist the brake, clutch

and speed-sensitive power steering, raise the
driver's seat (yes, really), lift the headlamp
pods, and very little else. True, this was
the first road-Maser with independent
rear suspension, but it's bog standard IRS
via double-wishbones, not Citroën self-
levelling, and the chassis definitely doesn't
settle when the power goes off.

Once you open the bonnet, some
differences do finally become apparent,
provided you can drag your eyes off the
sculpted, wrinkle-finish cam covers on that
big lump of V8. For one thing, it's a little
more crowded than Masers used to be:
the spare tyre lives under there, Citroën-
fashion, and likewise the power »

steering rack is right up top in plain sight. That leads me to notice something else, something Michael had told me about and isn't listed on your typical spec sheet: the engine sits way back in the chassis, behind the front axle line. This is technically a front-mid-engined car, a quality it shares not only with the SM but also with — guess what — the new Quattroporte. Maybe putting that Citroën hydraulic fluid into the Khamsin did introduce a little French DNA into the Italian gene pool after all.

Fortunately, when I slid through the driver's door, it was back to all-Italian again. Sorry, Citroën fanciers, but this is the way I think the interior of a fast car should look: big, round Veglia gauges, alloy-spoke leather-wrapped steering wheel, huge central tunnel with stubby shifter, the hand-brake lever from my old Fiat 124 Spider… hmmm, those keys seem familiar too:

Fiat 131? It doesn't matter; it all looks super, and with the exception of the silliest plus-two seat in the history of the planet it's also pretty comfy. Although I will admit it took a while to realise the hydraulic jack for the driver's seat was useless without the engine running.

With that I put the key in the ignition, push in the clutch pedal, and — bloody hell, I certainly hope we don't get stuck in traffic; I've felt lighter clutches on antique bulldozers. Find neutral (quickly), lift the left foot before it cramps, and spin the starter; the engine fires more easily than most others with a double downdraught Weber for each pair of cylinders and, after a few seconds, the glaring red eyeball slam in the middle of the dash goes out to signal the Bridge that Hydraulic Pressure has been Successfully Achieved and we may Proceed. Suddenly, the seat-jack not only works,

it's so eager that anyone over six feet had better be damn careful, or they'll put a Dan Gurney-style GT40 helmet blister in the roofline.

Right; I grit my teeth, grab the gear knob and give the clutch an almighty shove, promptly slamming it resoundingly against the floorpan. Ah yes — hydraulic power-assisted clutch actuation… something else that works much better with the engine running… oops, that's not first gear, is it, glad I didn't stall and sweet Holy Mother I sure got close to that gatepost… nobody was looking, were they?

A word of advice: take your novice Khamsin test-drive in a quiet, wide place with no distractions. The notoriously immediate Citroën power steering seems faster still in this car (Michael says it's because the front wheels sweep a wider »

*Right; I grit my teeth, grab the
gear knob and give the clutch an
almighty shove*

Khamsin debuted in 1972
replacing the Ghibli, it was the
first Maserati road-car with IRS

—

Manufacturers plate

—

Playing "catch me if you can"

Khamsin a fait son début en
1972 le remplacement de la
Ghibli, il a été le premier voiture
de route Maserati avec IRS

—

Plaque constructeur

—

Jouer "rattraper moi si tu peux"

Traditional Maser V8 is
powerful, flexible, and
sounds glorious

Moteur traditionnel Maser
V8 est puissant, flexible, et
fait un bruit magnifique

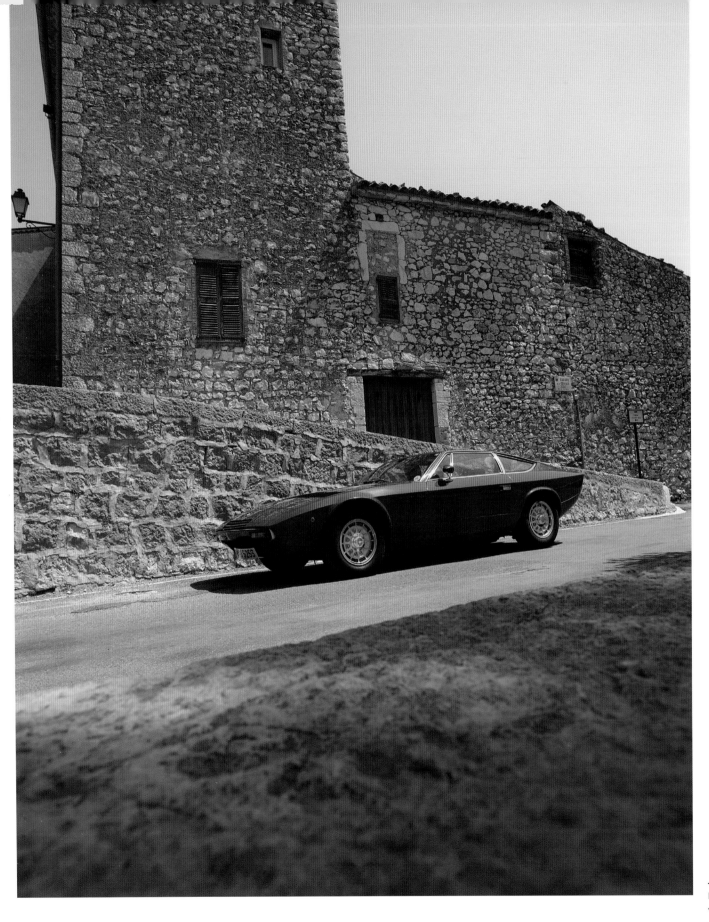

After all, I did turn around and drive it five times.
Not a real Maserati, my ass

Lunchtime in a sleepy hillside village

—

Unique glass panel between tail lights is surprisingly practical

Déjeuner dans un village dans les collines

—

Panneau de verre unique entre les feux arrière est étonnamment pratique

arc for the given amount of steering input); furthermore, the shift pattern is the cantankerous upside-down racing style, with first gear out of the 'H', and then there are the well-known Citroën zero-tolerance brakes. Add it all together, and somewhere in the first few miles you're simply guaranteed to make some sort of embarrassing mistake; it's a normal part of the learning curve. Sadly, it's probably also one more reason for the label "not a real Maserati".

Keep driving it, though, and the anxiety stage soon passes into a confidence stage, and ultimately leads to a downright cocky stage. Before long, I realize the engine has so much torque the first gear slot could very well be hidden in the glovebox for all

it matters — you only use it for starting off anyway — and that a high, firm, sensitive brake pedal with absolutely no free travel is exactly what I want for driving deep into the turns. As for the steering, I was sold the minute I took a hairpin without shifting my hands on the wheel, just like the in-car camera shot over M. Schumacher's shoulder. Add in the excellent neutral handling balance and a total lack of fussiness, and you can get attached to this car in very short order indeed. Meet it halfway, and it'll do anything in the world for you.

Then, on some out-of-the-way winding road I couldn't possibly find again near our photoshoot village above Cannes, I happened across this set of corners.

There was a tight, blind second-gear right, followed by a sweeping, open left-right-left, accelerating flat-out completely on through the lot with the car dancing gracefully along back and forth on tip-toes and an upshift in the middle, and back on the brakes hard, hard, harder and a blast on the throttle for the downshift for another blind right-hander and finally nail it up through third and fourth with all those V8 horses bellowing down the mountainside.

Well, yes, I should remember that part well enough, shouldn't I? After all, I did turn around and drive it five times. Not a real Maserati, my ass. ▪️

French bloodlines always show through

—

Modern road trips are sadly often more about the road than the trip

Lignées françaises sont toujours evidents

—

Malheureusement les histoires des trajets routiers modernes s'adresse souvent plus à la route qu'au voyage

FOOTNOTE

This was done on the same journey as the Quattroporte, as it was then closer to the modern era where it is common to generate copy for two or three articles per trip due to even tougher cost restraints. You do lose some spontaneity as the schedule can get very tight, and there is no time for a detour that may lead to interesting sidelines.

We did however get one gentle sunny lunch in the town square. Michael was really generous with his time and hospitality (and his magnificent wine cellar!) in helping us to do this feature.

The Khamsin is perhaps still not appreciated fully for bringing together the best parts of Citroën and Maserati. Contrary to hearsay, Giulio Alfieri, Maserati engineer and designer of F1 Grands Prix winning cars, stated in interviews that he had insisted on the Citroën hydraulics being incorporated in the Khamsin and other Maseratis of the era. In a meeting of the SM Club Italia, at which I was present and where Alfieri was guest of honour, it was very plain that he was immensely proud of the Maserati C114 engine that powers the SM and the Merak. He also answered all the questions put to him in the language of the enquirer, without a pause!

In my drives of Michael's Khamsin (gosh be careful) I found that it really is a superb Italian GT, smooth, quiet, and FAST.

—

ANDREW BRODIE 2012

The Unconventional Tourist

*The story of an unexpected American eBay bargain
and the classic French rally Tour Auto*

Words by Dale Drinnon
Pictures by Martyn Goddard

This very vehicle, you see, has just won the Tour Auto for Regularity

The rain is coming down in huge fat splatters now, the slimy French D-road nothing but a blurry grey smear framed by the windscreen, twisting through the trees and crawling up the mountainside. It is, of course, the perfect opportunity for the modern, 200+bhp, traction-controlled, anti-skidded, 4-wheel driven wundercar I've been following to shake this annoying old shadow from its mirrors. So that's exactly what the driver decides to do.

And he can't. A quick swipe at the gear lever and a stomp on the throttle and a gutsy exhaust howl sets in; the modern car up front stops getting smaller. At the first corner the chassis under me leans and leans and leans but absolutely will not fly off and by the exit I've clawed back everything he gained from his little breakaway attempt.

With the revs up, I'm no longer losing ground on the straights, either, and after a few more miles, both cars dancing around the turns in great streaming rooster tails and dashing along the humpbacked, wobbling tarmac between them in lockstep, we ease back to cruising speeds, contest ended. The big Citroën SM has successfully defended the pride of France and made me look like a hero.

All credit to the SM, that quixotic '70s intermarriage of Citroën running gear and Maserati power; my personal contribution to the cause lay mostly in knowing what the car could do and simply not getting

in its way. This very vehicle, you see, has just won the Tour Auto for Regularity, the time/distance class of one of the world's great classic car rallies, including the final timed section, held on this very road. Its long travel hydropneumatic suspension is perfectly suited to soaking up the mountain tracks that send hard-sprung, fat-tyred competitors skittering from one bump to the next; the crisp, torquey 4-cam V6 responds instantly and never causes a fuss. The SM, despite a reputation in some quarters as a gentleman's boulevard cruiser, can go shoulder to shoulder with an impressive array of machinery, new or old.

But the driver up ahead already knows that, he merely wanted to prove it to me in a way that would stick. He is Andrew Brodie, owner of this SM, and he has invited photographer Martyn Goddard and me to help drive the car back from France and sample some rally routes along the way. Our friend Andrew is a life-long Citroën enthusiast and the leading SM authority and tuner in the UK; ask him about the model and he'll be happy to tell you it's the finest Grand Touring machine ever built. In fact, he'll be equally happy to tell you if you don't ask him: it's one of his favourite topics.

For years he has felt the SM is tremendously under-appreciated, and when the chance to prove it against the likes of Ferraris, Porsches, Aston Martins, and the odd Lancia Stratos came along, he took the plunge. It was a bold move, especially on a very limited and largely self-funded budget;

Taking a gentle detour
returning from 2007 Tour
Auto victory

Un petit détour douce retour
apres la victoire du Tour
Auto de 2007

Doing it in a £900 car bought sight-unseen off eBay might seem downright hubris. Or worse.

the Tour Auto is the kind of event where some entrants use nice, clean new 100 Euro notes to wipe their dipstick. Andrew also had no previous rally experience, and to most people, an under-financed, novice British assault on a major international motorsport event might seem an obvious recipe for frustration.

Doing it in a £900 car bought sight-unseen off eBay might seem downright hubris. Or worse.

If truth be told, Andrew swears the whole project just sort of happened of its own accord. Tipped off last summer to a ratty SM in Seattle listed on the North American eBay site, he put in "a ridiculous bid, silly money, really; I bid $1250, which was

about 900 quid then, not expecting I had a chance, and forgot all about it…until I got an email informing me I'd won the thing, and I realized I'd better do something about getting it home…"

As purchased, the car was a runner but had a fried clutch, and with the additional complication of no automotive container shipping available from Seattle to the UK, the next step could have been a problem; fortunately, Andrew's years with the brand have made him well familiar to the loyal network of American Citroën devotees. Once he put the word out, offers of help came flooding in. The SM soon found its way across the US to New York Citroën specialist Dave Burnham, who made it self-propelled again, and from there to a

container ship bound for Andrew in London.

What he found he owned when it got there was something of a quandary: a high-mileage, mechanically tired car on its second engine, scruffy but sound, with no serious rust but lots of cosmetic troubles and missing trim; too nice to break up, but an expensive pain in the bum to put genuinely, truly right. In other words, the perfect candidate for a competition car. With the germ of an idea forming, Andrew called old friends (and SM enthusiasts, naturally) Bob and Ann Linwood about possibly driving the car in rallies someday. The Linwoods were regularity class winners of the 2006 Tour Auto in their own Alfa Romeo, and twice winners of the Tour

Drinnon and Brodie having
fun at Goodwood

—

Accelerating out of the
Goodwood chicane

Drinnon et Brodie s'amusent
à Goodwood

—

L'accélération en sortie de la
chicane Goodwood

En route to lunch

—

Maserati engine

—

Campaign badges

—

Interior with rally route map

En route pour le déjeuner

—

Moteur Maserati

—

Badges de campagne

—

Intérieur avec carte
d'itinéraire d rallye

de España. "I sort of said, you know, 'If I Build it, Will You Come?', and in a massive leap of faith, they said yes, and immediately suggested we enter the Tour Auto."

Preparing the car, Andrew says, was largely a matter of "just going through and fixing everything that was wrong". Tour Auto rules are pretty strict about period correctness, and in the SM's case, with few modifications homologated during its short original lifetime, that basically meant bog standard. A certain amount of interior stripping is allowed, so the carpets, sound deadening and rear seats were tossed: no real loss, the interior was rubbish anyway. The speedo could also be relocated to the co-driver's side to make navigation easier for Ann — but in the regularity class it has to be a standard production speedo,

not one of those fancy rally jobbies. Ann couldn't even use a digital stopwatch. Andrew installed ordinary fabric front seats, contributed by another SM owner, Jim Holyoake; fabric gives better lateral support than leather.

As for the engine, Andrew tore it down and inspected it thoroughly, then replaced all the bearings, valves, and a couple of cam followers, and bolted it back together. The gearbox needed no parts at all, only some adjustments.

Various other items had to be repaired or overhauled, the front subframe mounts, a door hinge, the electric windows, windscreen seals, lots of fiddly little bits. But very few involved actual replacement, and with the exception of the valves, gaskets, a stainless exhaust from P.D.

Virtually everything that went in was second-hand, to boot.
The paint, by the way, is also as it came, although considerable
time did go into spit and polish

Gough and rubber from Wembley
Tyres, virtually everything that went in
was second-hand, to boot. The paint,
by the way, is also as it came, although
considerable time did go into spit and
polish: Bob Linwood would never drive an
untidy race car, sponsors don't like them
any more than do scrutineers.

With the loan of a new C5 estate from
Citroën UK as a chase vehicle, and Barry
and Robert Lowdell of B.L. Autos & Sons
(who helped with the build-up as well)
joining Andrew on the support crew, the
team was ready to set off for France. The
start would be from Paris on April 24;
the total field of 272 cars, selected from
over 400 applicants, would spend five days
covering more than 2000 kilometres of
excruciatingly-timed precision driving.
A single wrong turn or flat tyre in the entire

five days, a few scant ticks over or under
the prescribed elapsed time would be
enough to blow the whole gig.

The other cars didn't have a chance, really;
Bob and Ann took the lead on the second
day, and never gave it up. Their cumulative
penalty time for the full distance was a
piddling 34 seconds, 18 seconds ahead of
second place; on three stages they were
dead on target. On one particularly nasty
section, Bob took a full half-minute from
an expensive opponent of exotic reputation,
but it would be most ungracious to name
any names, wouldn't it?

Not that the experience was totally
stress-free, a speedometer failure just prior
to the off necessitated an emergency call
to the SM Club of France. Two members
responded immediately, and as you might
be expecting from the Citroën faithful »

By a vineyard near Fleurie

A côté d'un vignoble près
de Fleurie

by this point, they also brought a car full of extra spares and a picnic lunch. Still, the replacement had a balky odometer and Ann had to do some clever re-calculating during each stage to compensate; the crew also replaced a noisy driveshaft at the end of day one, and a slightly iffy battery on day two, and… and that was it, actually, other than a splash of oil now and then. Which, in comparison to lots of other teams, was maybe rather stress-free after all?

Driving the car across the French countryside now is sort of like driving 125 percent of a standard SM; everything is the same, but better. Those famous qualities that make an SM so special, the wonderfully hard, sensitive brakes, the light, superfast steering, the sleek, distinctive aerodynamic lines, a superlative ride regardless of road surface, and yes, no matter how much True Believers hate the 'Q' word, the pure brilliant quirkiness of the beast, they're all still there.

And the SM's old curse, just that tiny touch too much weight, gets a world better if you throw out the interior. That suits me fine; the only drawback I can find is more of the lovely Italian growl when the marvellous Maser engine blasts you out of corners or gobbles up its next victim on the motorway, and somehow I think I could live with that. If the car has lost any of its civility, well, an SM has plenty to spare, and a full day behind the wheel still leaves you sad to turn off the key when it's over.

Nonetheless, in the end, Andrew Brodie is faced with yet another quandary. It's a fast, fun car, but motorsport isn't necessarily his thing and he's made his point; maybe he should sell it and move on. Then again, the Linwoods wouldn't at all mind driving it in the Tour de España this October. And they've won that twice before, you know… ▚

By a vineyard near Fleurie
–
Parked in the well known wine village

Un vignoble près de Fleurie
–
Stationné dans le village viticole bien connu

The winning Moment
—
Certification and club
badges
—
Dale Drinnon about to take
the wheel

Le Moment gagnant
—
Insignes de certification et
du club
—
Dale Drinnon au point de
prendre le volant

FOOTNOTE

After the Tour Auto, I had to drive the Rally SM home from the south of France, and was able to synchronise with Martyn and Dale for a run exploring Burgundy.

Our culinary highlight was a deluxe sandwich lunch after a long search, in a "closed" bar as it was a Fête Nationale. But I did manage to dive off into a Vente de Vin for an hour, to satisfy my curiosity and find something to bring home, while leaving Martyn and Dale at work.

Dale approached the Rally SM with caution but was soon happily throwing it around bends in the wet to please Martyn, while I looked the other way. Dale has since had some fun moments in the rally SM at Goodwood track days, and gosh he's a better driver than me!

In the Tour Auto, the expensive opponent thrashed over a special stage was a Ferrari. At the winning moment, however, the official cameraman swung away from the SM crossing the line to film a Ferrari passing nearby, so they did get their revenge.

We also learned the seriousness of the front runners in these major jaunts. On the second day, at 6:30 AM, the day's route map was not ready to be handed out as scheduled. Much wailing and "if looks could kill" from the front runners; they have the least time to assess the day ahead and some are out to win at all costs. Spectating and keeping up with the circus is a challenge; they do get a move on. Of course, some competitors fly home for the night in their Gulfstream!

Yes, the Linwoods did do the Tour de España in the SM — coming second equal after a stage that they aced was dropped from the scoring. And yes, they also did the Tour Britannia and came first there too! Their generosity in believing in the preparation of the car was very brave. Whilst no Ford GT40, the SM has shown it is not to be underrated in Competition, and I can think of no better car to campaign in Regularity.

—

ANDREW BRODIE 2012

Fortress and the Pont
Joly, Semur-en-Auxois,
photographed with Ilford
Delta 3200

Forteresse et le Pont
Joly, Semur-en-Auxois,
photographié avec Ilford
Delta 3200

Photo Notes

In Spring 1988 I was asked by Supercar Classics magazine to join Phil Llewellin on a road trip in Citroën SM-fettler — Andrew Brodie's metallic green example of the famous Franco-Italian grand tourer. Over the next nineteen years I subsequently recorded all the other adventures in this book as well, and used ever-changing choices in camera equipment and techniques.

The Nikon FM2 featured in the photograph is the one that I was still using when we set off to Normandy on that very first trip. I had favoured the lightweight compact SLR all through the 1970s as my everyday reportage camera for location portraiture and automotive action photography.

In the early 1990s I moved to the Canon EOS system to take advantage of their silky-smooth auto focus system, which was far superior to the Nikon alternative. The Canon EOS 1N was also extremely user-friendly when operating the various mode menus that were beginning to appear on professional cameras at that time. I was always looking for a new way of presenting a story and on the 'Charge de Gaul' trip in Andrew's DS19 I persuaded the Art Director of SCC to let me try a new Ilford black and white film called Delta 3200. I have always liked grain and the thought of shooting the story hand-held, free of a tripod, was inviting. The printers made a marvellous job in the magazine but it was the only occasion I ever used the film stock as its extreme contrast and lack of detail had limited appeal.

In 2003 I made the move to digital photography and have hardly touched traditional film since. For the 2005 story, the first after Phil's untimely departure, I used my state-of-the-art Canon EOS 1DS, then the pinnacle of digital weaponry

and £5,500 for the camera body alone. I still carried an old EOS film body for attaching a camera to the side of a car on a rig.

This was a wise move as Andrew Brodie, quite preoccupied with his duties at the wheel, scraped the perilously positioned camera along a wall on an Alpine pass while I was shooting a duelling Citroën SM and Maserati Quattroporte.

My aim is always to reduce the equipment I need, as in my view too much inhibits me as a photographer! My basic bag for these road trips contained the following:

2 camera bodies
17-40mm zoom lens
24-105mm zoom lens
80-200mm zoom lens
2 small flashguns
3 radio triggers
Tripod
Remote camera mounting rig
Reflector

—

MARTYN GODDARD 2012

143

Credits

This book was enabled by and we give thanks to:

MEL NICHOLS
Foreword

CHRIS MORROW
Translations

BETH LLEWELLIN
Allowing us to use Phil's words

**OCTANE MAGAZINE
& PRACTICAL CLASSICS
MAGAZINE**
Use of material

TILLEY ASSOCIATES
Design
www.tilleyassociates.com

GOMER PRESS
Printing and Binding
www.gomer.co.uk

**INTERNATIONAL WINE
& FOOD SOCIETY**
For education in wine and food
www.iwfs.org